In the Shadow of Empire:
Canada for Americans

In the Shadow of Empire: Canada For Americans

Joseph K. Roberts
Foreword by Leo Panitch

Monthly Review Press
New York

Map is based on information taken from the National Atlas of Canada.
© 1998. Her Majesty the Queen in Right of Canada with permission of National
Resources Canada.

Library of Congress Cataloging-in Publication Data

Roberts, Joseph K.
    In the shadow of empire : Canada for Americans / Joseph K. Roberts.
        p.   cm.
    Includes bibliographical references and index.
    ISBN 0-85345-996-7 (cloth). — ISBN 0-85345-997-5 (pbk.)
    1. Canada—Politics and government. 2. Canada—Foreign relations—United States.
3. United States—Foreign relations—Canada. 4. Canada—Foreign economic
relations—United States. 5. United States—Foreign economic relations—Canada. 6.
Canada—Social conditions. 7. Canada—Economic conditions. I. Title.
F1026.R66 1988
327.71073—dc21   98-13459
                                                                    CIP

Monthly Review Press
122 West 27th Street
New York NY 10001

Manufactured in the United States of America
10 9 8 7 6 5 4 3 2 1

Contents

To the memory of

Robert S. Lynd and H. H. Wilson,
socialist teachers

Foreword

A little bit of knowledge is a dangerous thing. Americans have come to know Canada a little better than they used to, but they still don't know us very well. In Atlanta during the 1992 World Series between the Braves and Blue Jays, the Canadian flag flew—but upside down. And at Yankee Stadium, "Oh Canada" was sung—but to the wrong tune.

Political misconceptions, based on a little—but not enough—knowledge, are sometimes no less bizarre. If it were just a matter of misconceptions among right-wing ideologues who think Canada is communist merely because of its refusal to cooperate in the embargo against Cuba, we might be able to rely on the satire of Michael Moore's film *Canadian Bacon* to set things straight. Sadly, even politically aware liberals and leftists hold a view that is almost a distorted mirror image of Jesse Helms's: Canada as some kind of social democratic paradise. When Clinton still sparked hopes that he would at least come through with a universal public health care program, it seemed as though every second commentator or politician in the United States was suddenly an expert on the Canadian system. And while the image conjured up by those on the right that Canadians spend most of their lives standing in line in the snow just to see a doctor was certainly mendacious, also misleading was the image painted by those on the left of how wonderfully fair and egalitarian life is just north of the border. You would almost think that Canada was Sweden. You would almost think that we can be whatever we like up here despite living "in the shadow of empire."

Joe Roberts's book is very timely in light of all this. It's about time somebody made the effort to say "Listen Yankee!" from the north side of the empire, to really try to explain Canada to Americans, and to do so while steadfastly criticizing those structures, attitudes, and policies within Canada that would leave this country as a "rich dependency" of the American empire. Himself originally an American, Roberts has been a stalwart socialist activist and intellectual in Canada, teaching at the University of Regina for more than three decades. A trenchant foe and uncompromising critic of American imperialism, he has also always worked hard to support the U.S. left, not least through his close association with the socialist journal *Monthly Review*. The contribution he now makes through this book, by helping establish a stronger analytical and informational foundation—a common fount of knowledge—for the alliances which need to be forged by the left across the 49th parallel, will surely be recognized as his most important legacy in this respect.

There are many facets of this book that will excite the reader's attention: its historic sweep; its analytic depth, its commitment to justice. Not least of its virtues is the sober and critical analysis it offers of the New Democratic Party of Canada and its forerunner, the Cooperative Commonwealth Federation. U.S. leftists, lacking a social democratic party of their own, all too often have overblown the strength and significance of the Canadian one. For example, the now-defunct Social Democratic Federation sent a tribute to the 1956 CCF convention which read, "Comradely greetings from the weakest socialist organization in the Western hemisphere to the strongest one. . . . It is a comfort to have a strong big brother next door to us." And today, a lot of Americans on the left attribute everything positive in Canada to the existence of the NDP—from our more militant and ideologically progressive labor movement, to the strength of the left intelligencia in the universities. This book celebrates those strengths and shows the real reasons for them, but it also explains the extent to which the NDP often actually undermines those strengths rather than fosters them.

In dispelling illusions about Canadian social democracy, this book may help clarify issues for the U.S. left in its work of renewing the labor movement and building new alternative political parties. The Canadian left needs Americans to make good progress on this. We can only hold out so long, only go so far without a change in the balance of forces in the heart of the empire.

Leo Panitch
Toronto 1998

Preface

As I grew up and was educated in the United States during the 1930s through the 1960s, Canada was opaque to me—some vast wilderness to the north, vaguely different but not threatening. Although some of my teachers were Canadian, and I had to learn something of the similarities and differences of Canadian, French, and American constitutional interpretation, I understood little else about Canada before experiencing it directly during the last thirty years.

It was once said that people on the U.S. East Coast absorbed the intellectual and cultural "truths" of Britain or Europe a decade or two after they were fashionable abroad. The flow is now of course in the opposite direction. But Canada was adopting fashionable U.S. norms only slowly when I first arrived. No longer. The pace of adaptation has intensified. The result is a penetration of values, standards, goals, and conventional wisdom in Canada today disturbingly like those of the hegemon to the south.

My account of what is different between these two neighbors is, in part, an attempt to help perpetuate the difference. For one thing, Canadians tend to describe their society as a "mosaic"; in the United States the more common term is "melting pot." The distinction implies that Canada cherishes the cultural differences of those who compose its fabric from one generation to another, whereas in the United States those of different origins are expected to abandon their roots and become part of a whole new entity. However distorting these mythic cultural ideals may be in both cases, there is at least the acknowledgement in Canada that there are enduring differences in the ways different groups see constitutional membership, identity, and therefore social purpose.

For both countries, however, after decades of mind- and politics-numbing Cold War, a new external justification emerged in the late 1980s to subordinate any domestic agenda for change. Under the title "globalization," international capitalist reorganization has arisen to justify liberating business and disciplining ordinary people and their needs. Communities and their governments must, so the dominant argument runs, recognize and accept the inescapable logical imperatives of international capital.

We possess no empowering grand theory with which to combat this spurious propaganda. Previous models for social reform in this century, however empowering in the short run, were ultimately self-defeating. Yet if we can agree that the human impulse to self-realization and group fulfillment remains as a social characteristic, perpetual subordination to a demonstrably illogical capitalism is impossible. Visions of transformation and experimentation with means of resistance have begun and will continue to emerge from the victims of capital. As Marx and Engels made clear, the conception of alternatives must be global quite as much as the problem is global. But the particularity of the struggle must start with the specific features of domestic, national contradictions.

The motivation of this volume is a wish to speak to those on both sides of the border about the pattern of U.S. domination and the ways in which Canada has succumbed to it in this century, with a view to developing a different kind of relationship and, at the same time, to alerting friends and allies south of the border that what appears normal about the relationship is not at all benign, enviable, or satisfactory. For concerned readers on both sides of the border, shared dedication to fundamental change is possible and necessary.

In this as in all creative efforts, many have contributed to the author's labors. My wife, Sheila, read and reread my drafts, making countless suggestions and corrections for which I am deeply indebted to her. Leo Panitch extended encouragement and invigorating advice throughout. He and Chris Roberts read the manuscript carefully and critically, suggesting useful revisions and correcting deficiencies. My colleagues Lorne Brown and James McCrorie generously supplied sources, corrections, interpretations, and encouragement. Paul Browne, board member of the Centre for Policy Alternatives, kindly supplied bibliographic data for me at short notice. Library personnel at the

University of Regina provided appropriate data sources throughout the research and writing process. The University of Regina provided the institutional support and, through collective agreement with the Faculty Association, the leave I needed to pursue this work. Finally, I am in debt to the Computing Services magicians and Crystal Sterzer, who saved me from this unforgiving new technology. Despite all this assistance and the care of my editors, I bear sole responsibility for any remaining errors.

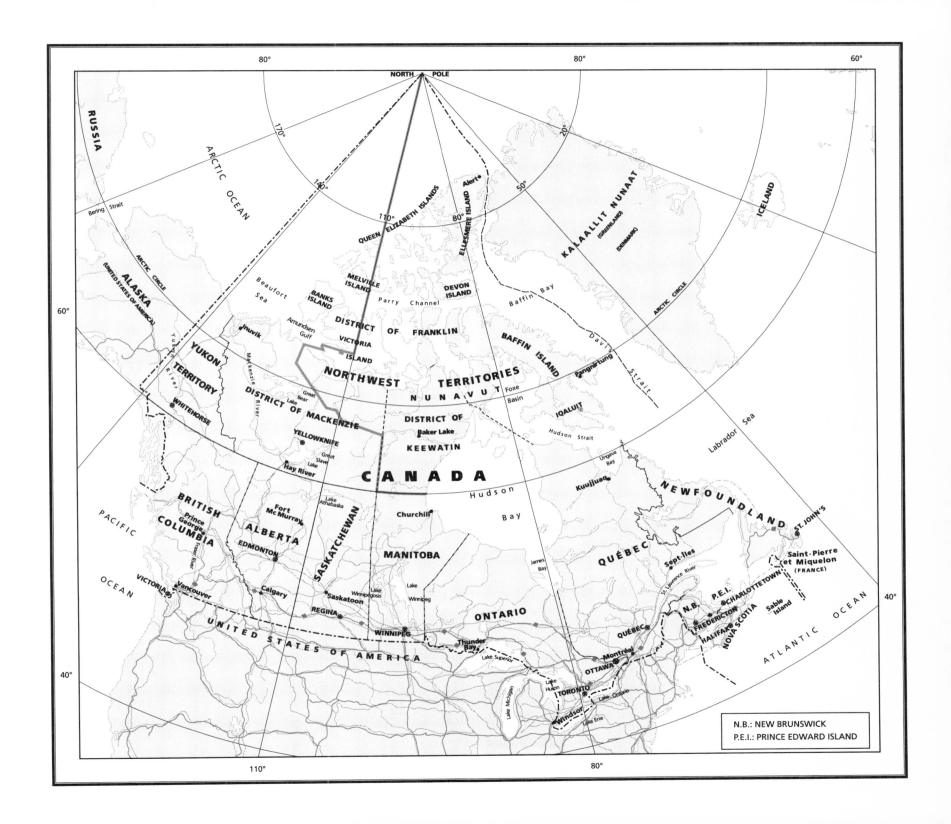

NORTH POLE

80° 80° 60°

RUSSIA

ARCTIC OCEAN

170°

Bering Strait

ARCTIC CIRCLE

ALASKA
(UNITED STATES OF AMERICA)

60°

140°

110°

Beaufort
Sea

BANKS
ISLAND

Amundsen
Gulf

Inuvik

QUEEN ELIZABETH ISLANDS

MELVILLE
ISLAND

Parry Channel

DEVON
ISLAND

DISTRICT OF FRANKLIN

VICTORIA
ISLAND

ELLESMERE ISLAND

Alert

80°

50°

20°

ARCTIC CIRCLE

ICELAND

KALAALLIT NUNAAT
(GREENLAND)
(DENMARK)

Baffin Bay

BAFFIN
ISLAND

Davis

YUKON
TERRITORY

Yukon
River

WHITEHORSE

Mackenzie River

NORTHWEST TERRITORIES

DISTRICT OF MACKENZIE

Great
Bear
Lake

YELLOWKNIFE

Great
Slave
Lake

Hay River

NUNAVUT

DISTRICT OF
Baker Lake
KEEWATIN

Foxe
Basin

Pangnirtung

Strait

IQALUIT

Hudson Strait

Labrador Sea

PACIFIC

OCEAN

BRITISH
COLUMBIA

Prince
George

Fraser River

VICTORIA

Vancouver

ALBERTA

Fort
Mc Murray

EDMONTON

Calgary

CANADA

Lake
Athabaska

SASKATCHEWAN

Saskatoon

REGINA

Lake
Winnipegosis

WINNIPEG

Churchill

MANITOBA

Lake
Winnipeg

Hudson

Bay

James
Bay

Ungava
Bay

Kuujjuaq

NEWFOUNDLAND

QUÉBEC

Sept-Îles

St. Lawrence River

ST. JOHN'S

Saint-Pierre
et Miquelon
(FRANCE)

40°

40°

UNITED STATES OF AMERICA

ONTARIO

Thunder
Bay

Lake Superior

Lake
Huron

Lake Michigan

TORONTO

Windsor

Lake Erie

Montréal

OTTAWA

Lake Ontario

QUÉBEC

N.B.
FREDERICTON

P.E.I.
CHARLOTTETOWN

HALIFAX
NOVA SCOTIA

Sable
Island

ATLANTIC
OCEAN

110° 80°

N.B.: NEW BRUNSWICK
P.E.I.: PRINCE EDWARD ISLAND

Chapter 1

North of the Border

The world's longest undefended border: this is how the relationship between the United States and Canada is commonly characterized. Like all successful ideology, this picture contains truth, but it also obscures reality.

Canada has acquired some visibility in the United States in recent years. In the debate over a national health plan, the Canadian single-payer system received favorable attention. The long existence of a left-wing New Democratic Party in Canadian politics has caught the interest of Americans. The continuing strength and social perspective of the trade union movement, which is proportionally more than twice the size of that in the United States, has earned respect. For many, Canada is attractive because of the explicit official support for the United Nations and peacekeeping, the apparent absence of nationalistic rhetoric, the lack of imperialist aspirations, lower crime rates, and relatively low levels of race conflict. This greater awareness of Canada is reflected in journals and debates with greater frequency since the advent of the Reagan era and since New Right politics took its hold on U.S. life.

For U.S. political and economic leaders, Canada has in this century seemed secure, cooperative, and inoffensive despite recurrent "trade irritants." Canada and the United States have the largest two-way trade in the world—approximately $300 billion annually—20 percent greater than trade between the U.S. and Japan.[1] To those with power, Canada seems not to be a source of trouble. Canadian leaders are inevitably obliging, particularly in matters of war and peace. To Americans, and to much of the world as well, Canada seems almost an extension of the United States. After all, the vast majority of the population speaks English. Even in French-speaking Quebec, people are more likely to speak English than Anglo-Canadians are to speak French; American tourists and business people are less inconvenienced by language in Quebec than they are in Mexico or parts of Los Angeles and New York City.

Despite Canada's attraction and accessibility, Americans have virtually no knowledge of the history of conflict and struggle that has brought about this society, which seems so American yet stubbornly insists upon its separate and sometimes hostile identity. Whereas the United States is ever present in Canadian learning, scant attention to Canadian history, society, politics, or economics is provided in U.S. schooling. There is little U.S. understanding of the domestic contradictions that have shaped Canadian identity and fuel present struggles.

Throughout its entire constitutional existence the development of Canada has been heavily influenced by the large and dynamic political economy to its south. Many Canadians have found work there. Colonies of Canadian "snow birds" escape winter in southern states. Prairie agriculture and settlement were decisively shaped by U.S. farmers and technology. Canada's vast natural resources have reliably supplemented the U.S. endowment. The two countries were allies in two world wars and have collaborated militarily and in war production since the 1940s. During the Cold War, Canada was a virtual cat's paw for U.S. military, economic, and diplomatic initiatives. Lester B. Pearson, it may be remembered, as external affairs minister and subsequently prime minister, won the Nobel Peace Prize in 1956 for his efforts to extract Britain, France, and Israel from the 1956 Suez Canal war against Egypt; in this he was encouraged and supported by no less a Cold Warrior than U.S. Secretary of State John Foster Dulles.[2]

Although Canada is in many respects not distinct from other advanced capitalist countries, its vulnerability to initiatives emanating from the United States is extreme. This is because of the very capitalist and liberal democratic fundaments, the similar institutions and values that define the social systems on both sides of the border. In the specifics of that relationship, the U.S. corporate ownership of much of the Canadian economy, the historic integration of the trade union movement, the adaptation in Canada to U.S. laws and governmental policies, the intimate working of the two military and police systems for half a century, the dominance of U.S. cultural content in the minds of Canadians—all these produce a kind of schizophrenic embrace of things

American even as they generate a deep suspicion of, even aversion to, many policies of the United States.

In short, the actual history of relations between and conditions within the two countries, the large and small instances of conflict, the national and class differences of interest and purpose, are concealed by the shared interpretation of an ideal relationship. But that idealized picture of dependable cooperation conceals a disequilibrium in attitude. Whereas Canadians live on a daily diet rich in information about the United States, Canada rarely becomes news in the consciousness of Americans until something so remarkable occurs as the Toronto Blue Jays winning the World Series. Nor do Canadians harbor attitudes of benign indifference, as their neighbors do. There is certainly great ambivalence toward the United States, but most Canadians resent the imperial condescension and arrogance of U.S. officials, whether directed against Canada or other nations.

One example of this ambivalence: the Clinton administration in 1994 attempted to enact gun control legislation but failed because of pressure from the National Rifle Association. In March 1995 the Canadian justice minister introduced comprehensive gun control legislation and was similarly faced with opposition from gun users. U.S. groups joined the campaign to defeat the Canadian legislation, which, however, went on to become law supported by popular majorities in every province, including those where hunters are most vocal. The attempted intervention by the U.S. gun lobby was not lost on the vast majority of Canadian supporters of the reform.[3]

Even the most ambivalent are dismayed by the smug self-satisfaction and patriotic bombast so deeply embedded in U.S. culture. There is also widespread fear and loathing of the more grotesque expressions of inequality and oppression in the United States, as well as the violent consequences. Many in Canada share the view of one commentator that their neighbor seems "riven by greed, corruption, distrust of government, litigiousness, a spiraling crime rate, and a prison population equal to that of a medium-sized nation."[4] Canadian political consciousness is wary of the United States in general and its governmental policies in particular. That unease becomes aversion on the question of U.S. control of the Canadian economy—a clear and present theme in Canadian political life since the 1960s. Canada has long been the preferred host for U.S. direct investment. (Territorially, Europe as a whole is in first place.)

How shall we understand this unequal relationship, this muted hostility? Why Canada's willing cooperation with an imperial project it nominally disapproves? Whence this cultivation of economic advantage that imprisons one beneficiary in a form of dependency?

Introduction to Differences

The inequality of the relationship is evident in a host of facts. Although Canada is second only to Russia in geographic size, its population is a tenth that of the United States, and more unevenly distributed throughout its vast territory. Most of the population is located in Quebec, Ontario, and British Columbia; most live within one hundred miles of the 49th parallel. The annual federal budget in Canada is $160 billion, that of the United States $1.6 trillion. The amount spent on the military in Canada is $9 billion (less than 6 percent) while it is $280 billion or 17 percent of the budget in the United States. Foreign (primarily U.S.) capital controls 44 percent of Canadian manufacturing and 42 percent of mining. U.S. firms control virtually all film and music distribution in Canada and are preponderant in publishing. In contrast, although overall Canadian investment in the United States rose from $12 billion in 1980 to $39 billion in 1992, including $1.3 billion in petroleum and $17.3 billion in manufacturing, there is no industry in the United States in which Canadian investment is preponderant.[5] Simply stated, U.S. capital controls the U.S. economy and Canada's as well.

Significant and increasing investment by Canadian capitalists in the U.S. economy helps explain the shaping of the Canadian economy and Canadian ambivalence toward the United States. For the loss of investment of Canadian capital at home is more than matched by the arrival of U.S. capital, or the reinvestment of profits earned in Canada, in a volume that results in U.S. control of major sectors of the Canadian economy. Aside from its access to Canada's great storehouse of natural resources, the United States has largely developed independently from the north, whereas Canada's economy, as a result of the great economic influence of the U.S. market and foreign investment, has developed as an extension of the United States in the twentieth century.

This decisive economic influence has also required the Canadian state to play a more determining social and economic role domestically than does its counterpart in Washington. With respect to this active state involvement in its economy, Canada bears some resemblance to late-developing countries such as Germany, though more accurately it retains the imprint of its colonial past, like so much of the third world. This reliance on an interventionist state is not attributable to a strong working class movement or ideology. The fact is that extensive use of nationalized industries and services for development objectives has been carried out primarily by bourgeois political parties. Only since the Second World War has Canada elected a few social democratic provincial governments which have nationalized public utilities and resource sectors as crown corporations.

Still, the extent of state-owned enterprise in Canada would be unthinkable in the United States. In order to manage the inevitable problems created by monopoly capitalism—uneven development, class conflict, environmental depredation, nationality and race relations—the Canadian state at federal and provincial levels has been required to redistribute income from wealthy jurisdictions to poor ones. It has been required to supply social wage supplements similar to those found in Europe. It has been required to provide a communication system as a backbone for the country without preempting private investment. These initiatives have produced a national social coherence and imparted a humane quality to Canadian society. Perhaps the most familiar example of the way the government has fulfilled the task of providing a social safety net is the national health program. The Canadian system was created in the 1960s despite intense opposition from the health industry, which was supported by its counterpart in the United States. The British Labour Party had introduced a comprehensive national health system in its first term in office after the Second World War. When remnants of the New Deal in the United States, together with organized labor and Henry Wallace's Progressive Party, attempted to do the same, the American Medical Association led the campaign to defeat the proposed legislation under the banner of preventing socialism as the Cold War and witch hunts gathered momentum.

Yet although Canada has achieved a level of social benefit which modifies to some extent the gap between social classes, Canadian history nonetheless includes a significant record of discrimination and injustice:

• *Women* in Canada have suffered from patriarchy, as in all societies. Only in 1929 were Canadian women deemed to fall within the legal meaning of "persons" and therefore become eligible to hold public office, a decision which at that time could only be rendered by the Privy Council Judicial Committee in London. The right of women to vote in Quebec was not achieved until the 1940s. But in the 1970s, a forceful, broad National Action Committee on the Status of Women was born, with significant consequences for the struggle for reform in Canada.

• *Indigenous peoples,* known in Canada as First Nations or aboriginals, who make up 2 to 3 percent of the total population and much higher proportions in sparsely populated regions, have been a "mudsill" fraction of society since the arrival of Europeans. A population of "mixed-blood" Metis emerged, serving the British and French colonial fur traders as cheap labor and as intermediaries with the full-blood Indians. The conditions of indigenous peoples generally worsened as settlement expanded and treaties were signed with the British and then Canadian governments in the later nineteenth century. They were relegated to reserves on marginal land, impoverished, subject to the paternalistic management of the Department of Indian Affairs, and denied political franchise for many years. Certain of their religious practices, language, and cultural traditions were prohibited, and their children legally abducted by white state and religious "welfare" agencies. Indigenous Canadians have only recently asserted themselves socially and politically.

• *Immigrants* have traditionally been restricted in order to preserve Anglo-Saxon and Francophone dominance in English Canada and Quebec. Some Chinese were imported to help build the railways in the nineteenth century; when that job was done, a head tax was imposed to prevent further immigration. In the early twentieth century eastern and southern Europeans and East Indians arrived in farming and mining communities, but never in the numbers experienced in the United States. Since the 1970s Caribbean migrants, East Indians, and now Southeast Asians have arrived to provoke the kinds of racist reactions in Canada that they have confronted in Britain, Europe, Australia, and New Zealand. Montreal, Vancouver, and Toronto have become zones of sharp conflict between white and nonwhite communities, with some of the same consequences for urban life as those familiar south of the border.

Tensions over these and other social inequities are increasing as the political economy adjusts to global restructuring and Canadian public policy conforms to the financial establishment's insistence on dismantling of social programs constructed between 1945 and 1980. Although the neoliberal and neoconservative programs under the regimes of Ronald Reagan and Margaret Thatcher have been analyzed and criticized by numerous authors, the impact of similar strategies on Canada were until recently less well understood, even at home. These policies were partly embraced by a Conservative Party government headed by Brian Mulroney between 1984 and 1993. Typical of their progenitors, the policies included benefiting the rich with tax concessions, rewarding friends with contracts, reducing social services, cutting state employment, deregulating everything demanded by business, privatizing publicly owned utilities and services and altering the political agenda to diminish other issues in favor of eliminating budgetary deficits and debt. The culmination of capitalist class success was the signing of both the Canada-U.S. Free Trade Agreement (FTA) in 1989 and the North American Free Trade Agreement (NAFTA) in 1993, despite the majority opposition as registered in popular opinion polls and elections. These were deals engineered to free capital from national state restrictions. Since adoption of the FTA in 1989 there are 365,000 fewer industrial jobs in Canada, a net reduction of 18 percent.[6]

The New Democratic Party (NDP), Canada's third major party, has been a powerful minority force expressing social democratic goals and challenging the dominant Liberal and Conservative Parties. As in the United States, strong local socialist parties and socialist labor groups existed in Canada before the First World War, but none ever grew into a nationwide organization. Also as in the United States, Canadian industrial relations were replete with violent strikes and lockouts. One consequence of the American industrial conflict was the legalization of collective bargaining by the National Labor Relations Act in 1935. Similar action was not taken in Canada until 1944, in response to a wave of bitter strikes during the war. Whereas the Roosevelt New Deal had attracted the activist elements of the labor movement, primarily the CIO, to support the Democrats, Canadian labor gradually became involved with the social democratic Co-operative Commonwealth Federation (CCF), which originated in a populist farm movement. In 1961, the CCF was converted to the NDP as the official political arm of the unified Canadian Labour Congress. Thus, while the AFL-CIO, lacking its own political voice, experienced the political decimation caused by business restoration and business unionism after the Second World War, the Canadian labor movement embraced a social democratic party strong enough to represent some of its interests in federal and provincial parliaments.

Canada's trade union strength has also made for a significant difference with U.S. society. As membership in trade unions in the United States has recently fallen to an estimated 15 percent of the paid labor force, Canadian union membership has varied between 36 and 38 percent, a size that gives force to its role in the economy and society. This reflects a contradiction. Canada is the only country in the world whose labor movement was dominated until the 1980s by the trade unions of a foreign country, but nevertheless pursued a different political course. Throughout most of this century the AFL and then the CIO moved into Canada and formed local branches of both craft and industrial unions whose head offices were in U.S. cities. During the 1960s and 1970s, public-sector workers organized in Canadian, not international, unions and fought aggressive catch-up battles. These unions became larger than the old established industrial, craft, and resource internationals, and they raised national and social issues at a time when the internationals were counseling caution, accommodation, and business unionism. In time, Canadian labor leaders were pressed to make the internationals more like the public-sector unions. In the 1990s, faced with shrinking membership and devastating demands for wage concessions, industrial unions have also converted their organizations to accommodate more explicitly to the Canadian national reality. It was this trade union movement, carrying a conscious economic nationalist perspective, that fought the Canada-U.S. Free Trade Agreement aggressively—but ultimately with no more success than American labor.

Yet the presence of a social democratic political party and a large unionized workforce has been insufficient to block the dismantling of the powers of federal and provincial governments that have made it possible to build an independent country. As opposition parties, the Liberals and the NDP opposed the Free Trade Agreement—yet once elected to office, they too accepted the neoliberal policy agenda and much of its ideological rationale, despite the palpable failure of that ideology and policy package either to solve the deficit issue or to alleviate the economic recession. The actions of Canada's liberal and left political parties are scarcely unique. The willingness of major parties to accept as "common knowledge" or "conventional wisdom" the neoliberal agenda of government cutbacks and reduced responsibilities is evident in all countries. The other side of the coin is that in the advanced capitalist societies, traditional liberalism of this century, social democracy, and the more radical socialists have all failed to assert an alternative economic and political conception of how to organize social life, including the market.

In Canada, an informal collaboration of the Liberal Party and the New Democratic Party was politically dominant from 1940 to 1980. In the 1990s that informal alliance gave way to a collaboration of Conservatives and right-wing populists. In this setting it should not be surprising to see signs of social collapse. Open racism is on the rise against Jews, immigrants, and indigenous peoples. Nationalism in Quebec produced a 1995 referendum on separation with results so close that many now believe a future vote will be won by the separatists. Conflicts over environmentally destructive resource practices are becoming angrier and more overt. Unemployment, for twenty years much higher than in the United States, in the 1990s rivals Europe at almost 10 percent nationally and as high as 20 percent in Newfoundland and 13 percent in Quebec. And as in the United States, even politicians have become sensitive to the hostility of the electorate to politicians and politics.

Understanding Our Differences Together

For progressives and opponents of the "business agenda," the struggle on both sides of the border is similar: to defend and strengthen those elements of the social tradition that enhance democracy and foster human cooperation; to resist the many forms of exploitation upon which capitalism is built; to envision and articulate alternatives to the prevailing "truths" that keep everything the same by denying that there are any alternatives.

Because of Canada's different history and different balance of class and national forces, however, its strategies and targets of struggle must also be different. The enduring colonial and then British imperial connection, replaced after the First World War by an overweening U.S. imperial influence, is perhaps the salient difference. The never-resolved contest between English and French culture, nationality, and power is certainly a different reality for the Canadian left, one that its American allies need not confront. This ethnic differentiation is distinct from the historic structure of racial oppression in the United States. (Both slavery and racism toward blacks are features of Canadian history, and the treatment of Canadian First Nations and American Indians is analogous, but Canadian slavery was never as extensive as the U.S. plantation system.) The Canadian ruling class, unlike that of the United States, functions as a comprador, historically acting as an agent and secondary beneficiary of imperialism; it has not itself been able to build an imperialist state or an imperialist ideology. In this respect it is relatively weak in relation to the needs and goals of the subordinate classes. This has made it possible, especially since the Second World War, to require the state to construct social programs, however incomplete and inadequate, more like those of Europe than of the United States. These differences condition the issues and strategies of struggle for progressive and radical forces in Canada.

Despite the immediately apparent similarities between English Canada and the United States, and despite continuing erosion through U.S. capital penetration of whatever distinctions exist, there remain important differences between the two societies. Most fundamental is the global imperialism of the United States, which has warped its own social fabric, particularly in the latter half of the twentieth century. Although Canadian capital willingly engages in that system, as does (more ambivalently) the Canadian state, one result of Canada's dependent status is a more generous public sentiment toward the worldwide victims of imperialism plus wide and deep disapproval of American global military adventures. Such sympathy helps account for a political culture of approval for the United Nations and its efforts. Similar attitudes and sympathies are not absent in the United States, but the contest against them there is great and real. That Canada has no military-industrial complex of the same economic and political magnitude as in the United States has meant a very different public conception of what is possible from public power than Americans imagine for themselves.

Another defining difference has been the French factor. Confederation, or the making of a Canadian nation-state, required the agreement of two founding nations, but the legal definition of Canada by the British North America Act involved a contract among elite representatives of several former colonies. This distinction remains inescapable as a political and social fact. The two founding nations still constitute a force restraining the centralization of power in the federal government. Reforms require the active involvement of the provinces, with Quebec historically playing a decisive role—sometimes in restraint, sometimes as initiator. This is why most sensible Canadians anticipate with real apprehension the potential separation of Quebec, which now looms in the foreground, making the English remnant (no longer culturally English) far more vulnerable to U.S. economic and cultural—and possibly even political—domination.

Canada also differs from the United States in its underlying assumption that the state (federal and provincial) is the ultimate repository of responsibility for providing social cohesion, improved living standards, and defense against foreign and domestic threats to these standards. The tradition of state intervention in the economy has characterized Canadian history in a manner similar to that of underdeveloped economies today and of all societies that historically embarked on capitalism and nation-state formation. But the positive social use of the state, although certainly not unknown, was significant in the United States only during the 1930s. There has never been a moment when the federal, state and municipal governments of the United States shrank from exercising their power for the needs and greeds of capital, but government officials have been far more indifferent about fulfilling the requirements of ordinary people. In American ideology, that is the responsibility of each individual.

Because of the broad and deep belief in Canada in the ability and duty of government to solve problems in the interest of social harmony, it has been hard for the neoliberal anti-state strategy to gain acceptance or legitimacy. Resistance to the destruction of old-age social insurance, the public health system, quality public education (including public funding for religious school systems), labor legislation, unemployment insurance, and many other social programs has been organized and powerful in all provinces and federally. At the same time, it cannot be ignored that this is an era of economic stagnation. Defense against destruction is all the left can at present contemplate. There is little in the way of new thinking about an improved society, let alone initiatives. Social democracy, the forum for many such initiatives in the past, has become part of the problem, an impediment to such reforms as are being demanded by popular organizations.

Finally, the free-trade-led restructuring of capitalism and imperialism was resisted earlier, more coherently, and with more continuing resolve in Canada than in the United States. The wounds inflicted in the struggle over the Canada-U.S. Free Trade Agreement continue to be aggravated by such incidents as the refusal of the U.S. forest industry to accept judgments favorable to Canada from dispute resolution panels on soft-wood lumber imports. International fishing disputes on both coasts continue without end.[7] The U.S. steel industry continues to act against Canadian imports. U.S. agriculture demands government action against imports of what it regards as subsidized

Canadian durum wheat. The powerful U.S. entertainment industry demanded and got changes to Canadian attempts at cultural protection: first the adoption of a law permitting U.S. ownership in broadcasting systems, then a successful challenge before the World Trade Organization of the Canadian law prohibiting split-run advertising. Congress demands that Canada, as a member of NAFTA, follow the U.S. lead in its obscene treatment of Cuba. The Helms-Burton Law punishing European, Canadian, and Mexican corporations doing business in Cuba has now assumed the proportions of an international trade conflict. In June 1996 a Cuban-American firm in Florida filed the first lawsuit against Sherritt International of Toronto, targeting profits from its Cuban operations under the extraterritorial law.

All such disputes point to the unwillingness of U.S. capital to submit to foreign competition that might endanger its markets, regardless of free-trade agreements. For a country like Canada that depends far more upon its trade with the United States than vice versa, such stories are national in significance and fuel nationalist animosity. At times that nationalism has been socialist; the right-wing version is no threat to imperialism. The status of dependency inevitably creates and recreates resentment because the relationship is not mutually beneficial, except to the capitalist class. Canada can never pose a threat to American autonomy, but the reverse is not the case.

The U.S. left is no less indignant than Canadians over the acts and attitudes of imperial arrogance, yet neither seems able to get beyond defensive reaction to each new outrage. More is needed from the left in the form of strategies for realizing alternative concepts of a future. Leo Panitch provided an example of such thinking in 1994:

> A 'possibly alternative state' to those sponsoring globalisation amidst competitive austerity . . . would have to be based on a shift towards a more inwardly oriented economy rather than one driven by external trade considerations. This in turn would have to mean greater emphasis being placed on a radical redistribution of productive resources, income and working time than on conventional economic growth. This could only be democratically grounded, as [Greg] Albo puts it, insofar as 'production and services [were] more *centered* on local and national needs where the most legitimate democratic collectivities reside.' Democratically elected economic planning bodies at the 'micro-regional' level, invested with the statutory responsibility for engineering a return to full employment in their communities and funded through direct access to a portion of the surplus that presently is the prerogative of the private financial system to allocate, should be the first priority in a programme for an alternative state.

This alternative could not be realised without at least some trade controls and certainly not without quite extensive controls over the flow of capital. [Panitch goes on to specify nationalization of banks.] Of course this would necessarily require interstate cooperation to install managed trade (rather than autarky) and to make capital controls effective. . . . International agreements and treaties between states will most certainly be required, but they will have the opposite purpose to the constitutionalising of neo-liberalism [which is how the free trade agreements must be understood]: they will be explicitly designed to permit states to effect democratic control over capital within their domain and to facilitate the realization of alternative economic strategies.[8]

However important the nation-state remains in any attempt by working people to recover even toeholds for a struggle against capital, today's issues are more international than ever before. If twenty-first century capitalism will be "global," so must effective resistance. This is why a U.S. left that opposes the dominant imperialism, and fights for the meaningful democracy that socialism was originally meant to achieve, must strategize openly with those in Canada (and others) whose struggles against capital should constitute encouragement and invite solidarity. We are, after all, bound inseparably in a common venture to try to transform the increasingly unacceptable capitalism that crosses our common border, undermining and devaluing our democracies.

Chapter 2

Canada's History, from Colony to Colony

The history of settlement in what is today Canada began in the "age of discovery" that we associate with Columbus.[1] John Cabot, exploring for the British government, came upon the coast of North America at either Cape Breton or Newfoundland in 1497. Like Columbus before him, he believed he had found China. Penetration of the northern part of the continent did not occur until Jacques Cartier made his way up the St. Lawrence River in 1535. But it was not until 1608 that New France was established by Samuel de Champlain. The French colony staked out along the St. Lawrence rivaled those coastal colonies being established in the same period by the British to the south.

But this vast wilderness initially appeared to be of little value. Since the wealth of the new world had been defined by the Spanish in terms of gold and silver, and since the economic mercantile strategy of capital accumulation focused on the amassing of precious metals, the absence of such wealth initially made New France unattractive. Nor was there any promise in agricultural plantations, for the glacially scoured Canadian shield contrasted sharply with the more verdant lands to the south.

The most attractive and important northern product was fish, particularly cod. Europeans fished the waters off Newfoundland and Nova Scotia long before settlements were established. In the sixteenth century, European demand for protein increased; the price of fish rose, and English, Breton, Portuguese, and Spanish fishing boats came in fleets to the abundant Grand Banks. Gradual changes in preparing and storing fish led to onshore settlements to process and dry the catch. In the seventeenth century, it was the

British who were most aggressive in setting up communities along the east coast of what came to be called the Atlantic provinces.

The commercial and military strategy the French developed in the interior was built instead on the fur trade. Relying on the network of rivers and lakes, they extended a linear system of trade westward and southward from the St. Lawrence Valley into the continental interior. The traders depended heavily upon indigenous aboriginal populations, particularly the Algonkian federation, to teach them the geography of the area and survival techniques, as well as the methods of capturing furbearing animals and preserving their pelts. By the decade of 1669 to 1678, the Mississippi River had been discovered and explored by La Salle for the French. This extended line of commerce required forts to protect and supply the harvest and voyageurs (boatmen and cargo canoe operators).

The British developed a counterstrategy to the overland system of the French. In 1670 they founded the Hudson's Bay Company to colonize the rim of the great tidal bay that extends from the Arctic Ocean deep into the continent. This gave the British a strategic position from which to enter the forests of the mid-continent without having to service an extended line of supply. Their fur trade was organized by two powerful mercantile companies—the Northwest Company, based in Montreal, and the Hudson's Bay Company, based in London—which meant wider commercial, and therefore military, rivalry between the British and French. Within a century this rivalry culminated in the French and Indian Wars, which were won militarily in 1759 by British forces under General James Wolfe at the battle of the Plains of Abraham at Quebec City on the St. Lawrence. The resultant Treaty of Paris in 1763 required the French to cede to Britain most of their territories in the Western Hemisphere.

At the same time that commercial rivalry was developing in the seventeenth and eighteenth centuries over the fur trade and the cod fisheries, agricultural settlement was proceeding slowly on three fronts. First in order of time and importance was that of the French colonists along the St. Lawrence River in what was then called Canada. The Company of New France was chartered in 1627 expressly to settle the territory according to feudal seigneurial practice. But feudal landholding and development was insufficient as a means of populating the new colony under conditions of marginal agriculture. When only seventy seigneuries had been conceded by 1663, Louis XIV revoked the company's charter, and the territory became a crown colony. The city and environs of Quebec, founded in 1608 on the north shore, formed the first locus; it was soon followed by Trois-Rivières and in 1642 by Montreal, farther upriver and deeper into the interior. The Crown awarded tracts of land to the seigneurs, who divided their seigneuries into farms or "roturs" stretching back from the river in long, narrow plots. Despite direct royal involvement, migration was slow; by 1712, only about 20,000 people lived in the colony. The rate of natural increase was high, however; in 1739, the census recorded 40,000 inhabitants, and by 1760 the population had increased to 65,000.

When the Treaty of Paris in 1763 ended the French regime, Canada was occupied by British troops, a British colonial regime was established, and the economy was commanded primarily by the British, who also became the dominant class of both Montreal and Quebec City. Although the majority of the population was Roman Catholic, the British rulers were Anglican. In 1791, Canada was divided into two jurisdictions: what is today the province of Quebec, then called Lower Canada by virtue of its location downstream on the St. Lawrence River, and Upper Canada, in what is today Ontario. At that time Upper Canada was still virtually unpopulated and thickly forested.

The second area of settlement occurred on the island of Newfoundland and what are today called the Maritime provinces: Nova Scotia, Prince Edward Island, and New Brunswick. Communites along the rocky east coast served as bases for the fishing trade and were typically made up of Scots, Irish, and west-country English, who retained their language and culture in enclaves. But the first agricultural settlements in the region had been established in the 1630s by French colonists who called their area "Acadia," centered on land reclaimed from the tidal flood plain of the Bay of Fundy in southwestern Nova Scotia. Despite the treaty of Saint-Germain-en-Laye in 1632, which granted Acadia to the French, British rivals continually harassed the colony and in 1654 seized control, driving out all but 350 residents. France regained control in 1670, and the colony again thrived and expanded. The geographers R. Cole Harris and John Warkentin comment that the relations between the Acadian settlers and the Algonkian Micmac Indians were particularly beneficial:

> Acadians became adept with birch-bark canoes and snowshoes and probably relied even more heavily on Indian lore about dyes, herbal remedies, and edible roots and berries than did the Canadians. As the Acadians perfected the techniques of farming the marshlands and agriculture became more important to them, the territory and economy of Acadians and Micmacs, although interrelated, became increasingly

distinct. Perhaps for this reason, the relationship between a European and an indigenous culture in Acadia was as harmonious as anywhere in North America.[2]

Acadia was captured by the English for the final time in 1710. In 1720, the French built a great fortified colony at Louisbourg on Isle Royale (Cape Breton Island) to control trade from the British colonies to the south. But the New Englanders were always able to evade French law and throughout the period traded effectively into Acadia. In 1755, with the onset of the Seven Years War, the British rounded up the Acadians and deported them to Louisiana and elsewhere. New England settlers moved in to take their farms and towns. Though some Acadians began to return in the 1760s, the culture they had created was all but destroyed. By the time of the American War of Independence, Nova Scotia was so extensively settled by New Englanders that many expected the colony to join the other thirteen in revolt.

The third region of settlement was in Upper Canada (what is today southern Ontario), along the upper reaches of the St. Lawrence and on the shores between Lakes Huron, Erie, and Ontario. At the time of the American War of Independence this was still densely forested and sparsely populated by Algonkian and Iroquois communities. But within eighty years, in 1860, more than a million and half people lived in what was called Upper Canada. In 1840, Upper and Lower Canada were reunited into a single administrative colony, as they would remain until Confederation in 1867, when they were divided into Quebec and Ontario of the newly independent Canada.

The settlers of Upper Canada were mainly from the British Isles and the United States, as Harris and Wartenkin note:

The Loyalists (Tories), who had arrived first, were dislocated by the War of Independence. Following them came the northern fringe of the restless, moving van of American land seekers—Pennsylvanians, New Yorkers, or New Englanders who had heard that prospects were better farther west and who eventually, perhaps after several stops found themselves in Southern Ontario. Then, and in larger numbers, came immigrants from the British Isles: Highland crofters, Glasgow weavers, Irish tenant farmers—all displaced in one way or another by agricultural, industrial or demographic changes. Some of them came out of tightly knit rural communities that had changed little over the years but far more frequently their roots in such communities were several generations back and quite forgotten. Most came to Southern Ontario as individuals or as members of nuclear families. A few, such as some of the Loyalists, had emigrated for political reasons; others, such as the Mennonites and Quakers, partly for religious reasons. But most came because they could not make an adequate living where they were. Often the more ambitious went directly to the United States or passed through Southern Ontario en route to the American Middle West. Those settling in Southern Ontario usually had been displaced by economic conditions in Britain and had nowhere else to go.[3]

Canadian settlement was different in important ways from the thirteen English colonies along the Atlantic seaboard. Mercantile chartered companies played almost no role for either the French or English in establishing settlements in the north, whereas they were key to the settlement of the Atlantic colonies. From the beginning, two linguistic cultures and two conflicting religions occupied distinct geographic jurisdictions, in contrast to the more homogeneous ethnic composition of the southern colonies. Canadian political unity was the outcome of a war between colonial powers, England and France, whereas the United States resulted from a successful revolt against colonialism. The northern settlements, unlike their southern neighbors, were neither slave-based plantation colonies nor, with minor exceptions in Nova Scotia and Ontario, religious dissenters' colonies. They were state-sponsored projects; for the English they were designed primarily to offset the French and to supply primarily timber, fur, and fish products to England.

After 1763, government in each of the colonies of Newfoundland, Nova Scotia, Lower Canada, and Upper Canada was entirely in the hands of the British Colonial Office, the military, and a commercial aristocracy located in St. John's, Halifax, Montreal, and Toronto, respectively. The settlers were primarily English, Scots, and Irish in the British colonies and French in Lower Canada, where rule was shared by the English with the Roman Catholic clergy. During the centuries of rivalry between the French and English, alliances had been made with different indigenous societies, which were variously recruited for military and commercial advantages. This colonial warfare, extending into the territory west of the Allegheny Mountains to the Mississippi River in what would become the United States, affected the evolution of Indians' lives for generations on both sides of borders they had not previously known.

The American and French Revolutions threatened the northern British colonial project. Northern settlers were recruited to military service against the revolting colonies. Loyalist slaves were promised land in Canada for their service. At the end of the war Loyalist settlers emigrated from the United States to Canada, much as third world revolutions today produce an exodus of landowners and capitalists seeking secure and profitable sanctuary. Often bringing wealth and farming skills, these Loyalists soon became prosperous landowners who agitated for greater popular participation in governance than ordinary colonial Canadians enjoyed. After the Constitution Act of 1791 the colonies of Upper and Lower Canada, Nova Scotia, and New Brunswick, where Loyalists settled, were managed by a governor appointed by the Colonial Office, an appointed council and an assembly elected on the basis of property, much like the representative governmental system of the thirteen American colonies before the Revolution.[4]

As H. McD. Clokie points out, however, the force of democracy released by the revolutions was too strong for the methods of traditional colonial control:

> Of the numerous difficulties in the colonial system, one [is] . . . of primary importance—the separation of powers between an appointed executive and an elected legislature. . . . In Upper Canada this was largely a contest between Americanised, non-conformist, frontier farmers and the High Church, exclusive, and ultra-loyal officialdom; in Lower Canada, it was a struggle between the small Protestant, commercial and dominant English official group and the conservative, French Catholic majority. In Nova Scotia and the other maritime colonies, the situation was similar to that of Upper Canada—a product of social and economic cleavages between the administration supported by old and well-established families and the assembly increasingly representative of the newer immigrants.[5]

In Lower Canada the consequences of the French Revolution were contained by the combination of British colonial government and Roman Catholic clergy, which controlled education, family, and community life. At the time, agriculture and rural life predominated in the colony, organized in feudal patterns of landholding and mercantile exchange. In Montreal and Quebec City the economy was almost exclusively in the hands of British traders and bankers. The colonial political administration too was in the hands of the English, except that an assembly with nominal powers represented the French-speaking "middle class" professionals. Since there were no state or business openings for this class, it was embedded as teachers, doctors, and lawyers in the largely peasant "Habitant" society of French Lower Canada.

By the end of the eighteenth century, great trading houses had arisen, specializing in the export of staple resources to Europe, especially furs. Yet even before the end of the century the fur trade was on the wane. In 1821, the Hudson's Bay Company absorbed its rival Northwest Company, extended its domain across the Rockies to British Columbia, and—until 1870—settled into the role of governor and landlord of the vast territory west of Lake Superior called Prince Rupert's Land.

In the latter part of the eighteenth century there was no bourgeois revolutionary ferment in the northern British colonies comparable to that in the thirteen colonies or in France. Yet during this period, as the effects of expanding capitalism were felt, rights for citizens (at least those with small capital) were demanded even before the extension of the franchise and democracy. In 1837, an uprising based on such demands did occur simultaneously in Upper and Lower Canada, an anticolonial insurrection led in the two jurisdictions respectively by William Lyon Mackenzie and Joseph Papineau. After two years of conflict, the revolt was defeated by the colonial military. Hundreds were killed in battle. Some 1,700 to 1,800 insurgents were imprisoned for high treason, and 32 were hanged. Several hundred were transported to the British penal colonies of Australia and Tasmania and hundreds more exiled to the United States. A further 25,000 were subsequently driven out of Upper Canada.[6] But despite the revolt's failure, the repercussions from it within Britain strengthened the Liberal Party's demand for an end to mercantile colonial policy. Soon the navigation and corn laws would be abolished and responsible government extended to the Canadian colonies in preparation for conditional independence in 1867.

From 1500 until Confederation, the development strategy pursued by the mercantile firms was to extract and export for sale in Europe the colonies' seemingly endless forest, sea, and wildlife resources. Since these firms were colonial companies built and owned directly or indirectly by British interests, the largest proportion of surplus value gravitated to Britain rather than swelling capital reserves in Canada. Capital formation did of course proceed, gradually. The banking establishment that today includes some of the major international multinationals, such as Bank of Montreal, Royal Bank, Bank of Nova Scotia, and Canadian Imperial Bank of Commerce, all originated in the trade of the St. Lawrence and Maritimes. But the agricultural surpluses along the limited arable lands of the St. Lawrence Valley, in the eastern townships of Lower Canada near the American border, and in the southern peninsula of Upper Canada found their way into British and American markets. Not until the twentieth century, with the settlement of the western prairies, did Canada produce a significant agricultural export staple, wheat, to provide a dependable annual balance-of-trade surplus.

Westward expansion and continental occupation became a conscious objective of the businessmen who crafted Canadian Confederation. Their strategy, called the National Policy, had three principal legs: construction of a continental communication and transportation system, a tariff to protect the new industry of central Canada, and the recruitment of immigrants to settle the interior. This protective and activist state policy was instigated by the Conservative (Tory) government of the first prime minister, John A. Macdonald, but was subsequently adopted by the opposition Liberals and endured until after the First World War.

The Canadian constitution of 1867, which established the federation, was actually an act of the British Parliament, the British North America Act. It was passed by a Liberal government as a result of heavy lobbying by a consortium of Toronto and Montreal bankers, lawyers, and traders. They reasoned that each individual colony was too small and weak to raise loan capital for industrial development, whereas a strong unified central government could guarantee such investment. In order to persuade the business communities of Nova Scotia, New Brunswick, and British Columbia to accede to the constitution, promises were made to establish a national market by building a railway system from the Atlantic to the Pacific. This the Canadian ruling class deemed necessary to thwart the continuous pull of the larger and richer American market.

The building of the Canadian Pacific Railway (CPR) was a far more monumental task than the profusion of private lines built by speculators in the United States from 1840 to the end of the century. To begin with, the population density or market potential of the enterprise was so insignificant that no private developer could be found to risk the expenditure. There had already been too much sour experience with Canadian railway ventures, culminating in the costly and unsuccessful Grand Trunk Railroad, a private venture requiring repeated state financing to prevent it from collapsing. As a result, the new federal government undertook the transcontinental feat, though it did so by funding a private speculator. In addition, the physical barrier was formidable. One thousand miles of rock shield, with dense forests and innumerable lakes and rivers, had to be crossed. The thousand-mile-wide prairies were not so difficult, but the final thousand miles—the Rocky Mountains, the succession of mountain chains in British Columbia, and the precipitate canyons of the Fraser River—presented enormous engineering and labor challenges. Work began in 1875, and the main line to Vancouver was completed in 1885. The company that built it received $106.3 million in cash and 44 million acres of land, including mineral and surface rights, from the Canadian government. Together with land rights retained by the Hudson's Bay Company, the CPR became a major real estate and therefore political power in the shaping of western Canada. Today it is regarded much as Rockefeller and Standard Oil are in the United States.

The territory of Prince Rupert's Land, which had been governed and exploited by the Hudson's Bay Company and included agricultural land of about 7 million acres, was sold to the Canadian government in 1869 for £300,000. This vast area was thus an annexed domestic colony administered by a Canadian governor as the North West Territory. In 1870, the province of Manitoba was created; Saskatchewan and Alberta followed in 1905. In 1949, the British colony of Newfoundland joined Canada to complete the ten-province Confederation. Today the area now called the Northwest Territories encompasses the region above the 60th parallel stretching from the Yukon to the Atlantic Ocean. The Yukon, bordering on Alaska, likewise remains a territory without provincial jurisdiction, a kind of domestic colony.[7]

Once again, in the 1860s as in 1837, the process of state creation generated rebellion among the inhabitants. Although fur and produce traders established an outpost as early as 1812 on the Red River at what is today Winnipeg, the population was overwhelmingly Indian and Metis. Under the leadership of Louis Riel the Metis and a few sympathetic whites seized the local government in 1869 and proclaimed an independent government. The federal government, lacking the physical means to crush the rebellion and fearful of annexationist agitation from Minnesota, reluctantly agreed to extend provincial status to the settlement; thus Manitoba entered the Confederation. In 1884, a similar agitation for provincial recognition in what would eventually become Saskatchewan was led by Riel, returned from exile in the United States. By this time the completed railroad in the Territories permitted the transport of federal troops who, armed with the new gattling gun, crushed the uprising and hanged its leader.

The second component of the National Policy, protective tariffs to promote industrialization, was conceived before Confederation but required a central government for enforcement.[8] The problem of tariffs might have led to North American integration as early as the 1850s: in 1854 the United States and

British North America entered into a Reciprocity Treaty, encouraging businessmen to believe that the future for Canada lay in integration with the United States as Britain withdrew from its colonial commitments. The U.S. government's refusal to renew that free-trade treaty after it expired in 1866, however, made the issue of protection for Canadian industry crucial. In 1879 the new federal government enacted a protectionist tariff, but even during the colonies' final phase, steep import tariff rates on manufactures were introduced in 1858 and 1859. From Canada's origins, therefore, the state actively promoted industrial development through protective tariffs, and this policy, in turn, interacted with the third leg of the National Policy: immigration.

The inducement of immigrants to settle on cheap land in the West began as early as the 1850s but initially met with little success: western settlement in the United States was still incomplete, the seasonal disadvantages of Canadian agriculture made the territory less attractive than land below the border, and most immigrants from Europe knew nothing of the particular demands of dry-plains farming. With completion of the railway, homesteading on the prairies was promoted by both the railway and the federal government as part of the National Policy. But only between the final decade of the nineteenth century and the First World War was there a rush to claim the land, and the greatest proportion of homesteaders were immigrants from the United States.

The National Policy became a bipartisan strategy for the creation of a Canadian market predicated on the export of staples such as timber and pulp, fish, and, at the end of the nineteenth century, wheat and industrial manufactures. But one of the results of the tariff policy was to attract American investment in manufacturing and natural resource industries, for once inside the British imperial system U.S. business could trade equally within the preferential barriers. American investors typically bought existing firms or established new ones as full owners, whereas British investors typically bought bonds, debentures, and stocks as portfolio investors. By 1922 U.S. capital had replaced British capital as the dominant force in Canadian economic development.

In the decades following Confederation, the Canadian state remained, as a Dominion, subject to British control in several areas. Ultimate judicial power lay not in the Canadian Supreme Court but in the Judicial Committee of the Privy Council in London until 1949. Cases arising out of the federal system, as conflicts over jurisdiction defined in the British North America Act, could finally be resolved only in London by judges with no experience in federalism. Nor could the Canadian Parliament amend its constitution without acquiescence of the British Parliament. In 1982, this situation was resolved with the patriation of the constitution. Canadian control of its own military and foreign policy was similarly subordinate to British will. Canadian entry into the Boer War and the First World War were determined by the British government. British citizenship meant full political rights in Canada, and Canadians were deemed to be British subjects. Not until 1931, with the proclamation of the Statute of Westminster, were the Dominions of Australia, Canada, New Zealand, Newfoundland, and South Africa accorded independence from British legislation, power over their own foreign policies, and full self-government. They were not to gain independent judicial power until 1949.

The Boer War at the end of the nineteenth century produced national conflict between French and English Canadians. When the imperial connection and British control of Canadian foreign and military policy sent Canadian troops to South Africa, Quebec objected to being recruited into a British colonial war. This objection would reemerge with the First World War in what became the greatest national crisis of the Confederation. The conflict over conscription can also be understood as the seed from which modern Quebec nationalism sprang. With Quebec's large population and correspondingly large parliamentary political representation, its politicians strenuously protested any plan for the conscription of troops to fight under British control in the war. Nevertheless, the Conservative Union government of Robert Borden in 1917 did introduce conscription and thereby nearly precipitated rebellion. The conscription crisis sealed the fate of the Conservative Party in Quebec until its rebirth under Brian Mulroney in the 1980s. A similar crisis was forestalled in the Second World War with a promise by the Liberal government not to send conscripts overseas; until 1944, Canada's military contribution in Europe consisted of volunteers. And even though the government won a plebiscite releasing it from its promise, the decision in 1944 to send all available troops to war produced a governmental crisis with defections among the Quebec's parliamentary delegation and the election in Quebec of the right-wing nationalist party Union Nationale.

From conquest (1763) until the twentieth century, the province of Quebec was dominated politically and economically by English-speaking occupants who came from both Canada and the United States. Excluded from business and urban employment opportunities, the largest proportion of Quebecois lived rural habitant lives and labored in extractive resource industries, primarily lumber. The Roman Catholic Church presided over their daily lives. By the twentieth century winds of nationalism began to stir, at first among intellectuals but increasingly in the provincial political process. The conscription issue was prominent in spurring this development. So were the beginnings of trade unions—at first creations of the Church—and then left-wing political parties, including the Communist Party, after the First World War stimulated secular and nationalist sentiment.

In Quebec, as in the rest of North America, the Great Depression of the 1930s was severe. It spawned a movement of workers out of the interior and into the cities. Wage-labor participation in Quebec manufacturing climbed from 152,502 in 1934 to 374,605 in 1943.[9] Unlike America with its New Deal, Canada did not establish innovative central government programs to deal with the economic collapse. The first reaction to the crisis by the Conservative federal government of Richard B. Bennett was to reaffirm orthodox nostrums of laissez-faire, followed by the rounding up of young unemployed men and their removal from cities to work camps in the wilderness, a militarized form of the U.S. Civilian Conservation Corps. Although this scheme was not imposed in Quebec, the Depression had a radicalizing effect in that province. Between 1931 and 1946, there were 667 strikes, climaxing in 1942 and 1943, when 133 and 103 strikes were recorded respectively. In response to increased political and trade union activism, the Union Nationale government of the province under Maurice Duplessis resorted to repression.[10] A figure reminiscent of Louisiana's Huey P. Long, Duplessis in 1937 enacted the Padlock Law, which barred access to any premises used for communist propaganda or any premises where communist documents were found. Nowhere was "communist" defined or specified. Provincial police for twenty years were able to persecute and outlaw any activity they deemed a threat to order.

In the western prairies, economic depression was worsened by a prolonged drought and wind storms comparable to those experienced in Kansas and Oklahoma. The provinces of Manitoba, Saskatchewan, and Alberta suffered agricultural devastation, and there was no salvation from local or federal governments. The export prices of farm products fell 70 percent between 1929 and 1932. In the same period average per capita income in Saskatchewan fell

72 percent. Throughout the region, agricultural income fell 94 percent (followed closely by coastal fisheries incomes, which declined by 72 percent).[11]

As in the United States and Europe, resistance to depression policies mounted. In 1935, the young men who had been conscripted into work camps in the western interior emerged to form an organized march on Ottawa in demand of real jobs and social support programs. Some of the leaders were Communists, but most were simply young people in search of meaningful futures. The Bennett Conservative government, fearing insurrection, ordered the Royal Canadian Mounted Police to stop the cross-country trek in Regina, Saskatchewan. A violent confrontation led to the death of one city policeman, the dispersal of the march and the fall of the Bennett government. Many of the trekkers subsequently joined the volunteers who went to Spain to support the Republican government against Franco's military insurgents. The battalion from Canada bore the names of the two leaders of the 1837 uprising, Mackenzie and Papineau.

In September 1939, when Britain reluctantly declared war on Nazi Germany, the Canadian response was not as instantaneous as in 1914. Prime Minister William Lyon Mackenzie King, knowing the sensitivity of Quebec as well as the increased independence conferred by the 1931 Statute of Westminster, stalled Canada's declaration of war for a week while he conferred with his cabinet and other politicians. As in the United States, war mobilization revived a depressed economy, put the unemployed to work, and brought millions of women into the paid labor force. But unlike that of 1914, the war of 1939-1945 bound the Canadian economy and government close to the United States. Military, diplomatic, and production planning and mobilization between the two countries grew closer during the Second World War. (The ensuing Cold War perpetuated defense-sharing arrangements, ensuring U.S. access to valuable mineral resources, air and naval bases, great-circle airspace, training, stockpiling, and information exchange.) Like the United States, Canada was spared the material devastation of Europe and Asia in the Second World War. But Canada lost more soldiers proportionally than the United States and emerged not as a world power but as a loyal ally. The processes of demobilization and conversion worked to contain the pressures for socialism that erupted in Europe, limiting Canadian social democracy and trade unions to dissent, criticism, and self-defense.

During the war, with memories still vivid of major confrontations like the 1919 Winnipeg General Strike, organized labor had grown rapidly and many large strikes had broken out. Even as the Depression-shattered economy returned to full production, by 1945 the social democratic Co-operative Commonwealth Federation party (begun by radical farmers in 1932) was threatening to defeat the federal Liberals on the wave of demand for reform of the political and economic system. As in most countries, the end of hostilities and return of veterans posed a social and political threat to the party in power. But the Liberals, always astute at bending before the winds of change, introduced Keynesian social reforms and legalized collective bargaining to usher in the great postwar compromise that saved the owning classes of Europe and the United States. The Liberal Party, with its policy of cooperation with U.S. capital and government, thus became the major political beneficiary of Keynesian strategy over the next thirty years. The CCF, too, advocated Keynesian policies of government economic regulation and stimulation of the economy along with mildly redistributive social programs. But it floundered electorally, unable to convert itself from agrarian populist radicalism into a European-style labor party.

Excluded from power during the postwar prosperity were the Conservatives, who retained a skepticism of the United States and a strong element of British loyalty. In their brief period of government between 1957 and 1963, when the party was led by the western populist John Diefenbaker, relations with the United States plummeted. Acceptance of nuclear warheads in North American Air Defense (NORAD) bombers on Canadian soil at the time of the Cuban missile crisis discredited Diefenbaker's regime and contributed to his government's defeat. Only in the 1980s, after adopting a continental strategy under the leadership of Brian Mulroney, did the Conservatives return to office long enough to adopt the U.S.-Canada Free Trade Agreement (FTA) and then the North American Free Trade Agreement (NAFTA).

The thirty-year era of capitalist growth and economic redistribution from 1945 to 1975, a period described as the social-democratic alliance or the compromise between capital and labor, did produce real social and economic benefits for a wide range of Canadian society. Women, indigenous peoples, new immigrants, and French Canadians—those who benefited least—found new voices. After 1960, women reentered the paid labor force in increasing numbers and many joined trade unions organizing in the public service sector.

These unions launched aggressive recruiting and bargaining campaigns to "catch up" with the wage patterns of blue-collar industrial unions. Politically, they organized the National Action Committee on the Status of Women, which remains a potent force to this day. In the 1970s, organizations of indigenous and Metis peoples began to form at provincial and federal levels and to denounce the policies and practices of the Department of Indian and Northern Affairs for its long history of colonial administration. The campaign to win back land stolen or alienated from Indians has since intensified, becoming a major political issue in Canada at the end of the century. Increased immigration from the third world since 1970 has resulted in the formation of ethnic organizations in the major cities of Canada. Their experience of discrimination in the major employment centers produced demands for changes in the always discriminatory immigration policies, as well as in local government and law enforcement.

But the most dramatic changes were those in the province of Quebec. After perennial subordination under conditions of conquest as well as domestically administered political and cultural repression, the Quebecois in 1960 launched a process of self-definition that has continued and, at the end of the twentieth century, challenges the entire Canadian Confederation. The repressive and reactionary rule of Duplessis's Union Nationale ended in 1960 with the election of a Liberal government that began a modernization and secularization process under the slogan, "máitres chez nous"—masters of our own house. Extensive reforms were introduced in education, health services, public finance, social programs, broadcasting, economic development, and more. For the first time French-speaking university graduates were recruited into top jobs in the public service, and pressure mounted for similar preference in the private sector. These social reforms inspired increasing challenges to the subordinate position of Quebec within Canada and demands for its independence or at least autonomy.

So intense did this movement become that in the late 1960s a small liberationist formation called the Front de Liberation de Quebec (FLQ) launched urban guerrilla warfare, including bombings and finally kidnapping and murder. At this point the provincial Liberal government appealed in 1970 to the federal Liberal government, headed by Pierre Trudeau, a Quebecois, to invoke the War Measures Act and send troops to occupy the province. This dramatic and ultimately traumatic action demonstrated to significant numbers in Quebec their continuing position as a conquered nation, and the Parti Quebecois was formed to lead the movement for separation. It has exchanged governmental office with the Liberals since 1976, always striving to mobilize voters around a strategy for separating the province from the rest of Canada. The original social democratic content of this nationalism has changed in the 1990s to a more conservative and sometimes racist ideology. The present leader of the party and premier of the province, Lucien Bouchard, was until 1989 a federal Conservative politician.

By 1975, the global retraction of capitalism characterized by stagnation of economic growth and mounting inflation signaled the end of Keynesian fiscal strategy and ultimately of the social compromise that had provided decades of relative social harmony. The federal government introduced wage and price controls, persuaded provincial governments to do the same, froze public-sector wages, and began reductions in public spending. But the more generalized neoliberal strategy of government deregulation, privatization, high-interest monetary restraint on the economy, and phobia about budgetary deficits was not introduced in Canada until the mid-1980s, some five or six years after Thatcherism and Reaganomics had defined the norm for Britain and the United States.

The 1980s ushered in the ideological, political, and economic strategies of "globalization," liberating capital and constricting the lives and prospects of the vast majority. This change has shifted the entire discourse of social and political possibility much further to the right than it has been since the 1930s. Even the interpretation of Quebec separation, radically advocated by the Parti Quebecois in the 1970s as an opening for socialism, is today cast in conservative and narrowly ethnic but thoroughly capitalist terms. The strongly economic nationalist sentiment of the 1960s and 1970s, which identified and condemned U.S. imperialism, stirs scarcely a mention in the political discourse of the 1990s. While Canadian trade union membership remains strong relative to that of the United States and even militant against universal cutbacks and high unemployment levels, the kind of progress experienced during the postwar decades is not even on labor's bargaining schedule. Canadian social programs, standard of living, optimism about the future, and sense of domestic security are under siege in the final decade of the second millennium.

Chapter 3

The Making of a Rich Dependency

Canada and the United States arose from a common colonial lineage, but the American War of Independence launched a different trajectory of development between the two countries. The U.S. Constitution was shaped from autonomous local struggles, especially between the merchant class and poor frontier farmers. Canada's constitution, a more explicit business contract among merchants, was legalized by the British House of Commons beyond the reach of the people. British, and then U.S., capital played a key role in determining how Canada would develop. In time Britain was forced into minority status, while the U.S. presence increased with the active collaboration of Canadian financial and commercial leaders. During the Great Depression, Canada did not follow the lead of the New Deal but did benefit, like the United States, from the restorative economic effects of war mobilization. The Cold War bound the two allies in a tight, unequal embrace, diplomatically and militarily.

In the process of shifting from British to American economic and political hegemony, Canadians were not inert; they did not stop struggling for an independent society. British capitalists had significant holdings in Canada, but they were portfolio investments (stocks and bonds) that could be and were traded to others, including Canadian financial interests. Canadian transportation interests, merchants, and industrial entrepreneurs in the nineteenth century also launched the cycle of modern capital accumulation within the newly created national market. At the time of Confederation, the Maritime Provinces (Prince Edward Island, Nova Scotia, and New Brunswick) were industrially the most advanced. Their subsequent impoverishment was one of the consequences of the political and economic restructuring toward western development that Confederation introduced.

The National Policy, the device of the new state to build an independent and integrated economy, was a conscious effort to secure the market for a class of domestic capitalists located primarily in Montreal and Toronto. Unlike the United States at the same time, the dominant element within this class of capitalists was not industrial but commercial; it was comprised of remnants of the mercantile trading system that had characterized Britain and France until the early part of the nineteenth century. Although industrial manufacturing did emerge in Canada in the second half of the century, various policies, including the National Policy, resulted in the encouragement of foreign, mainly U.S., capital investment in industry, whereas domestic Canadian capital concentrated in commercial, financial, and transportation development.

There were several flaws in this nation-building strategy. With Canadian capitalism built on mercantilism—that is, capital accumulation primarily from the circulation of goods and finance rather than from the manufacture of end products—a large part of the capital created in Canada reverted to Britain. More important, the dominant Canadian capitalists behaved as mercantilist commodity traders, primarily in natural resource staples. Financial capitalists, for their part, were not so interested in the risky, nascent industrial venture as they were in backing American investors whose Canadian holdings were tied to larger American corporations and markets. Soon after the National Policy went into effect and the steep tariff of 1879 was adopted, American investors found that they could buy existing Canadian companies or invest directly in manufacturing and mining ventures. In effect, they jumped the tariff barrier and operated like Canadian capitalists within a protected market offering preferred access to the international British imperial system.

The Canadian ruling class, from the beginning, was more cooperative than resistant in granting U.S. economic hegemony so long as the trappings of political independence and parliamentary sovereignty were respected. It was unnecessary for the United States to annex Canada (like Texas), purchase it (like the Missouri River basin and Alaska), or conquer it (like Cuba).

In the first instance, U.S. investors were attracted to the market in finished goods for the prosperous farming and resource industry workers. But unlike the British portfolio investments, which could be redeemed, plants and mines under direct U.S. ownership provided no real opportunity for Canadians to gain control of what Americans held. Thus, as a result of indifference to the question of ownership of the economy by the Canadian financial class, and the attractive effects of the tariff, U.S. capitalists chose Canada as their first effective imperial dependency—a rich one, in contrast to the colonies acquired in 1901 as a result of the Spanish-American War.

After the First World War, investment of U.S. capital in Canada rose rapidly and massively. In 1900 U.S. investment was estimated to be 14 percent of total foreign capital, compared with Great Britain's 85 percent. In 1922, U.S. capital topped UK capital by 50 to 47 percent. By 1930, the U.S. proportion rose to 61 percent, falling slightly to 60 percent by 1939, while UK investment declined to 36 percent. In 1945, the U.S. share of foreign capital investment in Canada was 70 percent, and it rose to a high of 81 percent in 1967 before falling back to 77 percent in 1970.[1] Canada was the largest single recipient of U.S. corporate expansion during the boom years following the Second World War.

As U.S. capital moved into Canada, it was perhaps natural that its opposite number, labor, would as well. Trade unions emerged in Canada in the 1840s and reflected the experience of their dominantly British members and leaders. As industry and the population grew, many Canadian workers found temporary or permanent work south of the border; this often entailed dual union membership. Starting in the 1880s, U.S. trade unions moved in to organize Canadian workers in the first instance of international trade unions in the world. This development of continental trade unions intensified from the 1930s through the 1960s.

The Role of the Military

In addition to the differences between Canada and the United States in capital accumulation, class formation, and state-building, there have been differences in the manner in which warfare has shaped the national experience, although the two states would become closely linked during the Cold War. Both countries were conceived in colonial conquest, repression, and rivalry. Seafaring piracy and brigandage made up a part of the early relationship between the two. But the U.S. conquest of indigenous people and military defeat of Mexico and Spain contrasts with postcolonial Canadian military experience, which was directed more toward fulfilling British objectives. Law and order were enforced in the Canadian West by a new federal quasi-military force called the North West Mounted Police, created in 1873, and the Canadian army was deployed in 1885 under British command to defeat the rebellion of Louis Riel, who sought an independent country in what is now the province of Saskatchewan. In the Boer War and the First World War, Canadian military forces were sent to aid Britain over the domestic objection of Quebec.

The transfer of hegemony from Britain to the United States was accomplished most completely during and after the Second World War. Canada formally coordinated war production with the United States under terms of the 1940 Ogdensburg Agreement, which created the Permanent Joint Board on Defense. In 1947, Canada formalized its military and strategic subordination to the United States with the Declaration on Defence Co-operation. This provided for the exchange of selected military and scientific experts and of observers for exercises and tests of materials of common interest; encouragement of common standards of "arms, equipment, organization, methods of training and new developments"; and reciprocity of "military, naval and air facilities."[2] In time a Distant Early Warning system of radar stations (DEW Line) was built and operated by the American military across Canada's high arctic and then a second Mid-Canada radar system (McGill Line) was built and operated by the Canadian military. Canada participated in the formation of NATO in 1949 and has remained an active member. In 1957 the Conservative government of John Diefenbaker signed the North American Air Defense Agreement (NORAD), which provided for "integrating Canadian forces into a defence system clearly dominated by the United States."[3]

Canadian forces were deployed in support of the American-led war in Korea (which was then represented as a United Nations action to deter aggression), but not in Vietnam—although Canadian military suppliers profited from U.S. defense contracts throughout that conflict. Canadian military intelligence officers joined their counterparts from Poland and India on the International Control Commission during the 1960s, a duty that included transmitting intelligence reports to the American military. In 1991, without any appreciable objection from the public or from opposition political parties, Canadian troops were mobilized to participate under American leadership in Operation Desert Storm against Saddam Hussein's Iraq.

An important part of U.S. defense strategy after the Second World War was to secure guaranteed supplies of vital raw materials. Canada is a most abundant storehouse of many such resources, including uranium. In 1952 President Harry Truman issued the Report of the President's Materials Policy Commission, called the Paley Report (after the commission's chairman, William S. Paley, president of the Columbia Broadcasting System).[4] The policy arising from this report would bind the development of Canadian resources deemed vital to U.S. defense closely to the needs of the capitalists, politicians, and militarists who waged the Cold War.

Diplomatic Deference and Resistance

In the United Nations, which Canadian politicians take much more seriously than do their U.S. counterparts, Canada has been as faithful to American leadership as it is possible for an independent country to be. Seldom does a Canadian ambassador to that international body stray from the line crafted in Washington. But there have been exceptions. Stephen Lewis, the former leader of the New Democratic Party in Ontario, was appointed ambassador in the 1980s by Brian Mulroney, the Tory prime minister. On several occasions Lewis differed with the Reagan foreign policy and publicly debated the merits of the UN with hostile spokespersons for that administration. On the issue of sanctions against apartheid South Africa, both Liberal and Conservative Canadian governments were more aggressive in their support than either the United States or Britain. Canadian leaders also resisted U.S. efforts to recruit them to the Organization of American States until the late 1980s, when Prime Minister Mulroney established Canadian membership.

Such defections are notable against a pattern of diplomatic conciliation. For example, in 1949, at the time of the victory of the Chinese Communist forces over the Kuomintang, Canada, like Britain, began the process of readying for recognition of the new government and establishing normal diplomatic relations. But when pressure against such normalization came with increasing intensity from Washington, the move was soon aborted. Yet as the Vietnam War crisis deepened in the early 1970s and President Richard Nixon undertook to repair relations with China, he successfully encouraged the Canadian government to extend diplomatic recognition to the People's Republic as a signal that China would be re-admitted to the community of nations.

In contrast to its loyalty to most U.S. Cold War policies, Canada has never endorsed the U.S. embargo of Cuba and has retained diplomatic relations with the Castro regime; thus Canadians can travel to Cuba and engage in some economic trade with Cuba. But the U.S. Congress has ruled that even foreign branches of American corporations are bound by U.S. embargo laws. Such extraterritoriality has forced numerous Canadian suppliers to refrain from filling orders from Cuba, and has caused Canadian governments since 1959 to treat Cuba coolly for fear of offending the United States. In March 1995, members of Congress demanded that Canada respect U.S. embargo policy against Cuba as an obligation under the Free Trade Agreement.

Another departure from the norm of collaboration came in 1983, when the Reagan administration decided to invade Grenada. The Trudeau government was known to oppose the use of force. As a result Canada was not informed until the invasion occurred, despite its membership in NATO and NORAD and its interest in the fate of a fellow member of the Commonwealth.

In diplomacy, then, Canadian dependency as well as occasional independence illustrates the relationship of perhaps the most developed and integrated form of modern imperialist relations. In order to retain at least a marginal position among the senior capitalist powers, Canada's ruling class has been attuned since the Second World War to the combined need to maintain legitimacy as an independent actor on the international stage while sustaining the endorsement of the United States.

Struggles for Cultural Independence

One of the most pervasive forces creating Canada's dependent capitalist society is the role of U.S. culture. The notion of hegemony, of course, implies the creation and reproduction of ideas, values, and attitudes to justify an existing power relationship. When Canada came into existence as an independent country, the dominant British culture gradually changed to reflect the particular physical, economic, and social circumstances of North America. Increasing Canadian interaction with the United States after the Second World War weakened the dominant Anglo-Canadian cultural tie to Britain, particularly in the Maritime Provinces, the prairie West, and British Columbia, and since then U.S. influence has become overwhelming. Much of the media, publications, music, and popular culture emanate from the United States and have now become a serious trade irritant between the United States and Canada.

As early as the 1930s, the U.S. cultural presence was so great that a Conservative government was persuaded that steps must be taken to ensure a national presence and a distinct cultural identity in the new broadcasting industry. Consequently, the Canadian Broadcasting Corporation (CBC) was created, with a French component called Radio Canada. A further state initiative established the National Film Board to ensure some presence in the movie business, although only in Quebec has a filmmaking industry independent of Hollywood succeeded.

So powerful has U.S. cultural influence become that a major debate erupted in English Canada in the 1960s over whether or not there existed a distinct Canadian identity. Since that time the seduction of commercial appeal and the volume of information have become torrential. Even if there is will to resist it, the means are now scarce. Beginning with language accessibility and shared bourgeois values, and extending to U.S. corporate control of the media and its contents broadcast across the border, English Canada receives a heavy diet of U.S. culture. The CBC maintains an important piece of the information and entertainment industry, but its existence is perpetually threatened by right-wing politicians hostile to state involvement in the media, as well as competition from private Canadian broadcasters, including media giants such as the Thompson conglomerate and Conrad Black's Hollinger network. In culture, as in all other aspects of the economic relationship, Canada is considered an extension of the U.S. market.

Yet as in other aspects of the domination, culture is not an uncontested terrain. Significant national forces have developed around such federal institutions as the CBC, the National Film Board, Telefilm Canada, and the Canada Council, which provides intellectual and artistic funding to sustain an independent culture. Here again the state has intervened to resist complete subordination of Canadian culture—especially in Quebec, where governments since the 1960s have played a major promotional role on behalf of cultural integrity in a manner similar to that of French governments. Further, most provinces have arts boards to distribute funds and services to artists, and many cultural workers are organized in professional organizations and trade unions. Even so, the financial lure of the vast U.S. market, and the prevalence of the idea that to "make it" in the United States defines success, have a perpetual corrosive influence on the artists and cultural industries of Canada. To make it in Canada, one must look like the U.S. product.

Virtually all film exhibition and distribution is controlled by American companies. The same is true of music recording and distribution. Much of the publishing industry is U.S.-owned. Television, video, and cable are dominated by American firms.[5] Recent examples of the force of U.S. policy on Canadian cultural institutions and practices include the Liberal government's sale in March 1994 of its majority share in Ginn and Company, the largest school textbook publisher, to the U.S. giant Paramount Viacom. Following a long-established tradition of state ownership in the economy, a previous Conservative government had intervened to acquire ownership when the company faced financial collapse.

In January 1995 the chief U.S. trade negotiator and enforcer, Mickey Kantor, invoked the Free Trade Agreement enforcement mechanism against an action by Canadian Radio-television and Telecommunications Commission (CRTC) which terminated the Country Music Television (CMT) cable network's programs in Canada (CMT is partly owned by Westinghouse). The CRTC regulation was intended to make way for Calgary-based New Country Network (NCN). At issue was the American contention that country music is simply a commodity, a business like any other, whereas Canada views it as part of the culture, which is exempt from the Free Trade Agreement. Under Kantor's threat of unspecified trade sanctions against Canada, a deal was struck in March 1996. The agreement gave CMT 20 percent ownership in NCN immediately and provided that the Canadian government would legislate permission for foreign companies to own as much as a third of any Canadian broadcasting operation.

Powerful American cultural industries such as film, represented by lobbyist Jack Valenti, have continually battled Canadian government attempts to protect culture. Although Canada's major political parties have promised to introduce legislation to facilitate Canadian film distribution, as a result of forceful intervention from the American industry none has been able to deliver such assistance.

For similar reasons, successive governments were until recently prevented from amending the copyright act to protect Canadian cultural production. For many years *Time* magazine and *Reader's Digest* were given free access to the Canadian market and even received the same production and distribution subsidies (awarded to Canadian publications until the 1970s) intended to give them an edge over U.S. competition. Later, *Sports Illustrated* discovered the technique of "split runs" to beat Canadian customs regulations by transmitting its publication via satellite directly to a Canadian printing plant. This permitted Time Warner to recycle the magazine, already paid for by U.S. advertisers and subscribers, in Canada and to resell advertising space at discounted prices—which crowded Canadian magazines out of the advertising market. In 1995, the Canadian government passed legislation banning the practice. But Washington formally challenged the legislation and postal subsidies before the World Trade Organization, which in June 1997 ruled in favor of the United States.

In February 1996, Ottawa intervened in plans by Borders, Inc., to move its giant book-retailing chain into Canada. The government agency Industry Canada discreetly advised the company that its planned expansion failed to meet the government's foreign ownership requirements. Borders withdrew its plans, which affected plans of Barnes & Noble, Borders's main competitor, as well—but it all proved a temporary setback, as Borders has now penetrated the Canadian market.

In the era of globalization, Canadian capital too is moving into the world entertainment industry. In March 1995, Cineplex Odeon Corporation bought Cinemark USA, Inc., creating the world's largest movie theater company, with 2,839 screens. Its aim is the domination of film exhibition not only in Canada and the United States, but in Mexico and Chile as well. Controlling interest is divided by Montreal's Bronfman distilling family and the Matsushita Electric Industrial company of Japan.

In its free-trade negotiations with the United States, the Conservative Party was moved by public pressure to exclude culture from the agreement. Many who work in cultural fields believe that this exclusion is not complete, and it is certainly true that the U.S. negotiators continued the fight to include culture in NAFTA and in the General Agreement on Tariff and Trade (GATT) Uruguay Round, where France also objected to the inclusion of culture. Those negotiations were concluded without a cultural properties agreement in December 1993.

The crux of this trade debate is that U.S. industries regard culture as a commodity, like toothpaste and automobiles. For the United States with its perennial trade deficit, cultural exports continue to be one of the most profitable sectors. For the establishment of U.S.-friendly consumer markets, culture has become an essential dimension of imperialism. But the culture of any national population is profoundly an expression of national integrity, beyond simple market measures. In Canada as elsewhere there is a continuing struggle between the universal capitalist content of "entertainment" and the integrating national, social significance of culture.

Ambiguous Nationalist Resistance

All these components of the Canadian social and political system reveal an incomplete national hegemony. It cannot be complete because both the structural class arrangements and the subjective ideological perspective simultaneously desire and construct a distinct society while subordinating Canada to U.S. domination and exploitation. A cross-class, nostalgic, and sometimes fervent assertion of "Canadian national identity" both coincides and conflicts with the continuing reach of the owning class to partake of profitable advantage in the U.S. or world market, regardless of the cost to Canadian autonomy. The class fraction that could be called a national bourgeoisie has never been strong and is at present virtually absent, unable to supply a vision of national purpose to unify an increasingly disparate population.

Public resistance to U.S. domination in Canada is not led by conservative and right-wing ideologies and parties, as it is in Eastern Europe, Germany, and France. On the contrary, the nationalist Parti Quebecois and Bloc Quebecois are strong advocates of free trade with the United States and look forward to Quebec's independence from Canada, confident that they can withstand U.S. imperialism. The right-wing populist Reform Party is similarly supportive of free trade and unregulated relations with American capitalism, believing them generally beneficial to small business and western Canadian interests (oil, timber, and agriculture). These political organizations object to the role of the Canadian state in furthering national culture and autonomous institutions and policies. Such a stance is not that of a bourgeoisie like those that have historically led countries to national independence. The Conservative Party, nearly destroyed in the 1993 federal election, once posed as the forum for national capital; that is, it formally opposed "continentalism," the strategy of the Liberal Party to cultivate trade and investment with the United States. But that posture was abandoned in the 1980s when the Tories adopted the same position that had long been espoused by the Liberals: an unrestricted opening to the United States.

During the decade of the 1980s, the small but powerful portion of Canadian capital that endorsed the neoliberal reversal on the role of the state faced the profound task of dislodging a political culture deeply committed to solving problems by encouraging provincial and federal governments to intervene creatively on behalf of stability in the social system. Historically, all Canadian classes, parties, and social groups accepted that role for government, though differing as to the extent and target of desired state action. That is, they supported an active role for the state in defining Canada as an autonomous capitalist society. But the ruling class, in its drive to curtail the power of the state to regulate and direct capital, has called into question the national definition of Canada.

Chapter 4

The Character of Canadian Classes

In both the United States and Canada, a small group owns the means of production and distribution, ownership that also accords its members dominant social and political power. The vast majority possess only their labor and intellect, plus personal goods, though when they organize in trade unions or occasionally in political movements, they can wield some power by virtue of their numbers or strategic advantage. Between the minority and the majority is a middle class with reasonable comfort and access to the amenities but little of the kind of power held by the owners of production and wealth. What is different in Canada is the structure that arises from the relation between the two countries. Canada is a dependency, and the United States is the greatest imperialist power in history. Canadian development is not completely self-directed, unlike that of the United States. As a result there are subtle but important differences in the composition of the classes and in the dynamic of their relationship.

The relationship of dependency between the two countries might suggest similarities between the Canadian class structure and class relations found in third world dependencies. Typically, such relations consist of a large population of technologically backward, impoverished peasants; low-wage urban and rural workers; and a small class of landowners in alliance with comprador commercial capitalists who are tied to the corporate and financial structures of the technologically developed metropoles. In contrast, however, Canadian dependency has developed despite a high-income working class and a skilled, prosperous, and (until recently) large agrarian class of family farmers, much as in the United States. What makes Canada resemble a third world dependency is the large amount of big capital investment controlled by absentee owners, mainly Americans, and managed on their behalf by a comprador class fraction tied to U.S. business.

The Canadian Capitalist Class

The Canadian capitalist class is made up of two fractions of big owners. The first, domestic owners, begins with the dominant sector of financial capital: ten chartered banks, trust companies, investment houses, insurance companies, and real estate developers, institutions owned almost exclusively by Canadians. To this group can be added some large merchandising companies such as Eaton's, breweries such as Molson's, some textile and clothing manufacturers, transportation and utility firms such as the Canadian Pacific Railway, a small number of heavy manufacturing companies such as Bombardier and Northern Telecom, and several diversified holding companies such as Power Corporation. Most of these owners are centered in Toronto and Montreal. Many are international players in the U.S., European, Asian, and third world markets. Unlike the United States and Europe, Canada has never had external colonies or economic dependencies requiring supervision by this class. Canadian capital since the Second World War has benefited from its association with American imperialism, but primarily as traders and financiers, not as initiators or administrators of imperialist relations and strategies.

The second fraction of Canadian big capital represent foreign ownership (American, Asian, and European), and dominates heavy manufacturing and resource exploitation (oil, minerals, forest products), typically through branch plants or subsidiaries of mainly U.S. firms. Foreign owners employ the services of Canada's managers, lawyers, and accountants; its media and advertising and public relations industries; and its academics and politicians. Taken together, these highly paid executives and advisers with the normal access to corporate stock rewards and other perquisites constitute the second fraction of the Canadian capitalist class. The members of these two fractions of capital ownership and control, constituting 1 percent of the population, are the ruling class. This class uses two political parties, Liberals and Progressive Conservatives, to accomplish their political purposes.

As befits a rich dependency like Canada, a numerically larger class of small capitalists flourishes in precarious uncertainty in agriculture, fishing, merchandising, the higher civil service, the professions, and service industries. Historically, the most important portion of this class was made up of farmers and other independent commodity producers. This was, during the formative years of the nineteenth and early twentieth centuries, a productive class that settled the West and supplied a surplus export staple, wheat, while providing a dependent but relatively rich domestic market for both U.S. and central Canadian manufacturers and suppliers. After the 1950s, as capital-intensive production reduced both the number of farms and the need for farm labor, this agrarian class of commodity producers went into a rapid decline. Since 1980, concentration of capital and aggressive harvesting of fish stocks have destroyed the Atlantic fishing industry and now threaten the Pacific Coast industry, hastening the destruction of that fraction of independent commodity production.

Settlement of the West and establishment of capitalist agriculture, as in the United States, required appropriation of the land from the indigenous peoples who occupied it. The vast herds of bison were slaughtered. Treaties imposed upon the native populations removed their claim to the land, converting it to private property and relegating the occupants to reserves paternalistically administered by the federal government and North West Mounted Police. Thus segregated and marginalized, indigenous peoples were held in thrall until the revival of their political consciousness and activism in the 1970s.

The western agrarian class on both sides of the 49th parallel in turn found itself exploited by and dependent on big capital as represented in the Winnipeg and Chicago grain exchanges, the grain elevator companies, equipment franchisers, and the railroad and shipping companies, as well as the banks. As a sector of small capital producing a large supply of a homogeneous staple, farmers sold into a world market over which they had no control. Prices were determined anonymously by supply and demand or, more precisely, by middlemen—traders and shippers—while the manufactured supplies and loan capital they required were monopoly-controlled, hence priced according to what the market would bear. Both Canadian and U.S. farmers built populist movements in the late nineteenth and early twentieth centuries to fight the monopolies. In Canada they established a vast network of retail cooperatives, wheat pools, and credit unions. But farmers also required political strength, which led them in the 1920s and 1930s to create both right- and left-wing populist parties: the Progressive Party, the Co-operative Commonwealth Federation, and Social Credit.

The Working Class

Although there are many similarities between American and Canadian capitalist development and therefore between the formation of the working class in both countries, there are differences that have affected the balance of class forces past and present, as well as working class consciousness and solidarity. Canada's working class evolved within an incompletely autonomous society as a high-wage, largely ethnically homogeneous labor force in the separate English and French jurisdictions. Both the American and Canadian processes of industrialization faced a relative labor shortage, which resulted in high wages; but unlike the United States, Canada had no large freed slave population which could be counterposed to the white working class, and thus used to confuse the development of class consciousness. In Quebec, the urban working class of the nineteenth and early twentieth centuries was predominantly immigrant, primarily Anglo-Saxon; the rural and resource working class was amply supplied by a high Francophone birth rate. Late nineteenth- and early twentieth-century Anglo-Canadian immigration policy ensured that non-British, European entrants would be directed to the agricultural settlement of the prairies.

Uneven development of Canada's dependent capitalism also accounts for a class development different from that of the United States. Canadian heavy industry was first developed and then destroyed in the Maritime Provinces during the nineteenth century. Industry was then reconstituted in southern Ontario and Montreal in the nineteenth and early twentieth centuries, producing a concentration of the working class there and in the resource-extraction hinterlands. Single-industry (fishing, mining, logging, and pulp and paper) towns, scattered across the country in isolated sites, were often incubators of class-conscious organization and militant confrontation with British and American owners.

Given the proximity of the larger and more dynamic economy to the south, Canadian workers enjoyed relative mobility to seek U.S. jobs. Many European immigrants to Canada also moved on to the United States in search of jobs, often to stay but sometimes to return. Outmigration was particularly characteristic of French Canadian loggers moving down into New England in the nineteenth century.

This fact of labor mobility and, of course, capital mobility resulted in the formation of cross-border trade unions. In the 1880s, the Knights of Labor were actively organizing workers in Ontario. The Knights were crowded out by Samuel Gompers's American Federation of Labor (AFL), which began to sign up Canadian craft workers, thereby insuring the freedom of members to work either side of the border. In the western forests and mining camps before the First World War, the Industrial Workers of the World (IWW) and the Western Federation of Miners (WFM) brought a militant, class-conscious form of organizing into British Columbia and Alberta from Montana and Idaho.

The AFL went on to organize extensively in Canada's areas of industrial concentration. The first Canadian federation of unions, the Trades and Labour Congress, formally affiliated with the AFL in 1903. But the leadership of the AFL advocated craft organizing. Syndicalist and industrial unions, such as the IWW, the WFM, or the One Big Union of western Canada, competed and contended with the AFL, as they often did in the United States. In 1937, autoworkers in Oshawa, Ontario, invited the new Committee (later, Congress) of Industrial Organizations (CIO) and the United Auto Workers (UAW) to help them organize the U.S.-owned industry in Canada. The UAW, its hands full organizing the big three automakers in Michigan, lent advice but little else. Ontario's political and economic leaders nonetheless saw the cross-border cooperation as a communist invasion and reacted violently. By the Second World War, most Canadian industrial trade unions were branches of international unions with headquarters in the United States, just as most of Canadian industry was a branch of American capital.

Early on, Canadian trade unions recognized the need for a political vehicle. The AFL's Gompers was opposed to union involvement in politics, preferring "to reward friends and punish enemies." But most Canadian union leaders of the time, having come from the British labor movement, accepted the need for an organized political voice. After the First World War, the Trades and Labour Congress and the rival All-Canadian Congress of Labour both attempted to form labor parties. There had been regional socialist parties with strong ties to labor, primarily in the West, since the turn of the century, though none affiliated with the Second International, the worldwide gathering point of social democracy. The Socialist Party of British Columbia, one of the earliest and strongest, became the Socialist Party of Canada in 1904, modeled on Eugene V. Debs's Socialist Party of America.

The First World War immediately conscripted Canada in support of its imperial parent, and the attendant adoption of the War Measures Act—which suspended normal constitutional practice and allowed the government to rule by decree—led to a broad range of mobilization regulations, including curtailment of union activity. By the end of the war, workplace tensions were high. The ensuing Winnipeg General Strike of 1919 sparked other major strikes, such as in Quebec, frightening the ruling class. The state moved quickly to confront the threat of insurrection. The federal government, which had already begun adopting internal security measures, now amended the Criminal Code, making it "a crime punishable by up to 20 years in prison to belong to any association whose purpose was to bring about governmental, industrial or economic change by force or which advocated or defended the use of force for such purposes."[1] Summary deportations of resident aliens during the early 1920s took place simultaneous to the Palmer Raids in the United States, the notorious federal crackdown on radicals and immigrants.

The 1917 Russian Revolution generated broad sympathy among Canadian socialists and trade unionists, and the Winnipeg General Strike further sparked revolutionary aspirations. In 1922, a handful of socialists in Ontario founded the Canadian Communist Party (CP), which was soon admitted to the Third International (Comintern) centered in Moscow. One early and exceedingly effective CP initiative was the creation of the Workers' Educational Association, later the Workers' Unity League (WUL). The WUL was the most energetic and successful union-organizing influence in Canada during the Depression, until it was abandoned when the Comintern turned its focus to building the less militant antifascist Popular Front after 1935.

This very success brought the CP into conflict with the AFL as well as with the newly founded Co-operative Commonwealth Federation (CCF). After the birth of the CCF in 1932, the social democrats among the many union leaders of British origin became members and, toward the end of the 1930s and during the war years, engaged in bitter contention with the CP. Communist analysis in the late 1920s and early 1930s irresponsibly identified social democracy with fascism. CCF and moderate labor leaders' hostility toward the CP intensified in the late 1930s as the CP vacillated from advocating unity of antifascists, to opposition to wartime preparations in the face of the Hitler-Stalin pact, to all-out support for an Allied victory after the Wehrmacht attacked the Soviet Union. Comparable internecine conflict in the labor movement occurred in the United States and Britain.

The Cold War produced the same campaign against domestic Communists in the labor movement as occurred in the United States. Indeed, the anticommunism and atomic spy hysteria that swept U.S. politics from the late 1940s through the 1950s began with spy-ring revelations in Canada by defecting Russian diplomat Igor Gouzenko. The purge of Communists from the labor movement was carried out in Canada mainly in the international industrial unions, primarily by CCF trade unionists, whereas in the United States the government led the purge. By 1955, the power of the Communists in the trade union movement was broken, and the social democrats were freed to concentrate on solving their other problem: electoral anemia.

The trouble was that western farmers, but not industrial workers, supported the CCF. The party's officials, led by labor lawyer David Lewis, decided that a British-style labor party would have to be created without repudiating the western farmers. Toward this end, the CCF was to be replaced with a New Democratic Party (NDP) which would be christened "the political arm of labour." To set the stage for this transformation, the two labor centrals, the Trades and Labour Congress and the Canadian Congress of Labour, were merged in 1956 to form the Canadian Labour Congress. This happened about the same time as the merger of the AFL and the CIO in the United States, but the outcome with respect to labor politics was significantly different.

Following the NDP's inauguration from the ashes of the CCF in 1961, it was hoped that not only union officials but members as well would swing their support to the new party. On the federal level this has not occurred. But at the provincial level, which has regulatory jurisdiction over most union-management relations, the NDP has exerted considerable influence in both government and opposition. This is important in Ontario and British Columbia, where labor is concentrated. In Quebec, the NDP is insignificant, but the Parti Quebecois exerts an ambiguously pro-labor influence on the long-ruling Liberal Party. In the early 1990s, NDP governments were elected in British Columbia, Saskatchewan, and Ontario on platforms that committed them to reform labor legislation. The scope of these reforms, though decidedly less ambitious than supporters were led to expect during the elections, have extended some legislative protection to unions and workers.

Changing Labor Realities

The Canadian working class is numerically smaller than that of the United States, but exhibits greater organizational strength in its trade unions. While the proportion of nonagricultural workers in trade unions is higher than in the United States, however, unemployment in Canada has run at 10 percent or higher during the late 1980s and 1990s, whereas U.S. unemployment is normally at 7 percent or less.

On the threshold of the twenty-first century, the working classes of North America and Europe are being fragmented and reconstituted by the relentless restructuring of international capital. For example, in contrast to the overwhelmingly male workforce of yesteryear, women today make up 45 percent of the Canadian paid labor force. Further, what used to be a predominantly Anglo-Saxon labor force is now much more ethnically varied as immigration has brought labor power from Asia, Africa, and Latin America. This process is recognizable in all developed capitalist societies. In the 1990s, job creation has shifted away from secure, lifetime occupations to casual, temporary, and short-term employment. Permanent, full-time jobs are held by only 58 percent of the Canadian work force; the rest are seasonal, part-time, and temporary. Between the advent of the Canada-U.S. Free Trade Agreement in 1988 and the end of 1995, Ontario lost 400,000 jobs. In the Ontario auto industry, a major engine of economic vitality, General Motors alone reduced jobs from 35,800 to 29,700 between 1988 and 1993. By October 1995, thirty-seven of the largest corporations, the main advocates of free trade, had cut 215,414 jobs.[2]

North American and European capitalism has changed profoundly since the 1960s, altering the balance between the manufacturing sector and the service sector. The heavy industrial manufacturing component of the Canadian labor force has shrunk in proportion to the service component. Beginning in the 1960s, more and more white-collar workers were brought into the collective bargaining system. An increasing proportion of these were women. By the 1980s, the largest unions in Canada were in the public sector: the Canadian Union of Public Employees, the National Union of Provincial Government Employees, the Public Service Alliance of Canada, and the Canadian Union of Postal Workers. In addition, traditional heavy-industry unions such as auto and steel were increasingly organizing membership in ancillary and unrelated industries: fishing, office work, and services such as fast food. Coincident with these shifts in the composition of the work force and its organization was a conflict over strategy and a rising nationalism among Canadian union leaders.

Trade unions in the United States fell before the devastating onslaught of capital's counterrevolution in the 1970s and 1980s. Wages were curtailed or rolled back, concessions on hard-won contractual rights were demanded and won by management, right-to-work laws were passed in many states, and union membership fell precipitously. U.S. branch plants in Canada demanded the same kinds of concessions, and some leaders of international trade unions accepted the advice of their American parent bodies. But others rebelled at the prospect of rolling back gains made over long years of struggle, most notably in the United Auto Workers. Strategy differences with the Detroit leadership led, in 1986, to the withdrawal of the Canadian autoworkers from the UAW. Subsequently, other international unions split along national lines, and even those that retained their international structure, such as the United Steelworkers of America (USWA), have extended greater autonomy to their Canadian branches.

A further impact on the labor movement came with the Canadian state's attempts to control the surge of inflation in the 1970s, which marked the change from a policy of collective-bargaining consent to state and corporate coercion of labor. In 1975, the federal and several provincial governments introduced mandatory wage and price controls which lasted for three years. In 1982, a subsequent "guideline" of 6 percent and then 5 percent maximum wage increases was enforced in the public service. The effect for two to three years was to remove a third of Canada's organized workers from the collective bargaining process to determine conditions of work and the right to strike. Further, since 1970 there has been a sharp increase in government-legislated back-to-work measures to end annoying strikes.[3]

In the face of a worsening environment for organized labor, a part of the labor movement—exemplified by USWA leadership, but also including some voices from the left and the social movements—have embraced "progressive competition"—that is, the argument that by cooperating with corporate efforts to strengthen Canada's ability to compete internationally, it will be possible through economic growth and state administrative practices to maintain and extend social programs currently facing the budgetary ax. Others on the left, along with leaders of the Canadian Auto Workers (CAW) and some other unions, reject the idea that Canada's political integrity and social programs can be protected by embracing business competitiveness. That logic, they hold, would inevitably destroy the principles of community and solidarity on which social programs depend. As two CAW research officers put it:

> In the competitive model the target is the individual firm. In a model whose goal is the democratic development of productive capacity, the focus is on sectors or on clusters of firms within sectors. . . . [The] determination to work locally, the focus on production networks, the need for co-ordination and planning, the regulation of corporate investment, the recognition that economic activity is a social process, and the opportunity to strengthen labour—combine to make democratic development possible and to provide opportunities for workers and popular action. In the competitive model these opportunities are summarily foreclosed.[4]

Despite the restructuring attack against organized labor by Canadian capital, the balance of class forces in Canada has remained more favorable to labor than in the United States. This is due to several factors. Most important is the uneven development of the economy. Employment in the tertiary (services) sector is proportionately greater than in primary (extractive) and secondary (refining and manufacturing) industries. Union membership that was lost through capital-intensive mechanization and organizational restructuring in the primary and secondary sectors was made up in the tertiary sector. Through the 1970s and early 1980s these unions provided momentum to the Canadian labor movement as they militantly sought to catch up with industrial wages, although recent attacks on public-sector employment have stayed this advance.

A second factor in Canadian labor's relative strength derives from the fact that Canada is an export-oriented economy, again in contrast to the United States. Owners can ill afford protracted disputes that imperil exports of both primary and manufactured products. It is also true that the subjective willingness of Canadian labor to strike determines the behavior of export-oriented capital. Until the end of the 1980s, among the countries of the Organization for Economic Cooperation and Development (OECD), only Italy experienced more lost time due to strikes than Canada. In the 1990s, however, that frequency of strikes dropped sharply, reflecting workers' falling expectations.

Third, the Cold War did not decimate socialists in the Canadian trade union movement so effectively as in the United States. Many can still be found in union leadership, and the existence of provincial NDP governments has supplied some legislative and administrative sympathy for labor from time to time.

Racial Divisions among Workers

The divisive effect of racism is central to any understanding of the working class experience. Unlike the United States, Canada has very little heritage of African slavery; instead, class conflict has been mediated in part by manipulation of the French Canadian "race" issue. A small number of former slaves were granted liberty and land in Nova Scotia for their loyalty to the British cause in the American War of Independence, but these Loyalist blacks fared no better in Canada than American blacks in the northern states. In the early twentieth century, a small number of freed slaves came to western Canada to settle as farmers, but their numbers were so slight as to pose no threat to the white settlers. The Chinese workers who were brought to Canada in the last quarter of the nineteenth century to build the transcontinental railway were discriminated against and ghettoized much as in the United States. At the turn of the century, a head tax imposed on Chinese immigrant workers effectively prevented their families from entering Canada, and the Chinese Immigration Act, passed in 1923, which excluded Chinese immigrants, was not revoked until 1947. During the Second World War, Japanese-Canadians in British Columbia, like Japanese-Americans on the West Coast, were rounded up and put into internment camps, their property confiscated.

But the most abiding racial dimension of the Canadian class system is formed by the indigenous population. During the fur trade of the eighteenth and nineteenth centuries a class of low-wage workers was created through the intermarriage of British and French males and Indian females in order to create a "half-breed"—Metis—labor force on the frontier. Historically, this population has been treated by whites as Indian, but the state deprived them of the legal status of "treaty Indians" who received reserve "privileges" and related funding. As a result, Metis who did not find a livelihood as trappers in the deep bush have lived a largely urban ghetto existence, experiencing all the traumas of capitalism's very poor.

In the 1980s and 1990s immigration from the third world has somewhat diluted the dominance of the two charter (French and English) ethnic groups. Migrants from the French-speaking Caribbean, Southeast Asia, and Africa have entered Quebec, some with enough capital to qualify as small entrepreneurs or professionals, and some as political refugees. But most are former peasants or workers seeking economic security and opportunity who generally find marginal and insecure employment as taxi drivers, domestic workers, food workers, hospital orderlies, and similar service work. Montreal in 1991 had a poverty rate of 22 percent, the highest in Canada. A corresponding influx from the larger English-speaking third world has entered the work force of the nine Anglo provinces in the same categories. In addition, wealthy economic refugees from Hong Kong escaping the prospect of unification with China flooded into Vancouver and Toronto during the 1980s, generating a decade of real estate boom and speculation.

But a restrictive immigration policy has prevented these new populations from assuming the size and concentration in Canada that American cities have experienced. Although they alter to some degree the dominant English and French white ethnicity, especially in the large cities, the populations are smaller, and the culture of racism does not have the historical and structural features, or the same degree of viciousness, found in the United States. With the exception of indigenous people, who do experience historic, institutionalized racism, most new immigrants from the third world have not until now been subject to institutionalized discrimination. Since the 1970s, however, the black communities of Montreal, Toronto, and Halifax have suffered dramatically at the hands of trigger-happy and overwhelmingly white police forces; as elsewhere, these communities have organized to protest and demand changes. But in an era of stagnant high levels of unemployment and the attack against public services, there is some evidence to indicate an ominous development of more widely dispersed racism, informally coordinated through networks similar to those found now in Europe.

Basic Similarities, Important Differences

Despite the similarities of the U.S. and Canadian class systems, their main difference is in Canada's dependent relationship to the United States. Subordinate classes in the United States reflect to this day the racial origins of U.S. capitalism as well as the autonomous development of the richest imperialist society the world has ever produced. In neither of these experiences is Canada equivalent. The Canadian ruling class has historically been relatively unconsolidated and vulnerable to social movements arising from small business and independent commodity producers, from organized workers, and from Quebec sovereigntists. As late as the 1960s, independent commodity producers in agriculture and fishing could still exercise strong minority political influence through their own parties, whereas U.S. subordinate classes have not had their own ideological or political vehicles for most of this century. Canadian subordinate classes have typically sought self-protection and a reasonable share of the economic pie, though not social transformation. The organized strength and self-consciousness of the working class and popular groups allied with them has curtailed but not prevented the exercise of power by the Canadian ruling class. One measure of the balance of class forces in Canada lies in the fact that the dominant class is not organized to project onto an international scene an imperialist project with all the attendant implications of state financing, strategy, diplomacy, administration, and enforcement.

The specific history of every capitalist nation-state is the product of many diverse conflicts and resolutions, most fundamentally that between social classes but also those between genders and nations. One important unique feature of Canada when compared to the United States is the continuing cultural and ethnic conflict between Francophone and Anglophone nationalities. The long record of struggle between these two charter nationalities affects class conflict and all other aspects of Canadian life. Understanding the history and current expressions of the conflict is crucial to understanding Canada.

Chapter 5

Quebec's Quest for Nationhood

The fact of a French-speaking nation in North America is an abiding reality that English-speaking Canadians, much less Americans, have never thoroughly grasped. While the United States liberated itself from Britain and then expanded its territory by destroying indigenous peoples and buying and annexing land, Britain was busy creating Canada in part by conquering a rival French colony and appropriating its territory, as well as that of indigenous peoples. Since the Second World War, Quebecois national consciousness has reemerged ideologically, politically, and constitutionally, with sometimes violent results. At the same time, economic and social class development since the 1960s has created in Quebec the conditions for a possible independent nation-state, peacefully achieved. Such a step would dismantle a classic national market dating from the era of liberal capitalism.

With its large, ethnically dominant, and nationally conscious population, Quebec constitutes a major political force in Canada; achieving a majority bloc in the federal government requires major representation from Quebec. Despite such political weight, no Quebecois held an important economic portfolio until the 1960s, and the province supplied no finance minister until the late 1970s. The 1995 census estimates Quebec's population at 7.3 million in a Canadian population of 30 million. (Nearly a million more ethnic French live in the rest of Canada; in New Brunswick, descendants of the Acadians constitute the second largest ethnic group and exert significant political influence.) The Canadian census of 1991 reports that 5.6 million in Quebec claimed French as their home language. The English-speaking population of Quebec, some 600,000 in 1991, is a mere 9.2 percent of the population. Other linguistic minorities accounted for 8.8 percent.

After the English conquest and occupation of New France, the right-wing nationalism of the French clergy and petty bourgeoisie suited the English merchants well enough because it was exclusive and introverted. Economic and political power remained in the hands of an English-speaking minority. Quebec was acknowledged as a province under Confederation, and ministers from Quebec were included in federal cabinets after 1867; it was not accorded any status different from other partners to Confederation. The importance of this point is that Quebec is the home territory of a defeated nation, in its colonial form. The thirteen original American colonies joined in a successful war of national independence and were, in that enterprise, equals (except for size, which required the main compromise upon which the U.S. Constitution rests). In contrast, Canada has throughout its history failed to acknowledge the national identity and the difference between Quebec and the rest of the signatories to the British North America Act.

Sovereignty and Separatism

The Quebecois have not just been excluded from power and privilege; they have resisted assimilation, like much of the indigenous population. Thus, in the 1960s and 1970s the movement for national development and autonomy in Quebec, which includes the assertion of national identity, presented a fundamental power challenge to the Canadian ruling class.

At the beginning of the twentieth century, as national self-confidence increased, two concepts of national purpose developed in Quebec. The first advocated a two-nation Canada of equal status: French and English. The second, repeatedly put forward by reactionary nationalists, advocated making Quebec the sole repository and defense of French presence in North America and espoused autarkic development. But neither strategy succeeded in generating independent capitalist development because, until the 1960s, economic power and even final political power remained in English hands.

The renaissance of the 1960s produced two ideological and strategic camps in Quebec. The provincial governing party has generally been the Liberals, whose strategy is development within Canadian federalism. The opposition to the Liberals, made up of both right-wing and left-wing nationalists and separatists, has governed for several periods from the 1960s on. From rural peasant and urban proletariat before the 1960s, the class character of Quebec has changed to encompass a fully urban, organized working class, an educated administrative and professional stratum, and a small agribusiness class. More recently there has developed a small fraction of large, independent capital, part of which supports separation.

Beginning in 1960, the Quebec Liberal Party under Jean Lesage pursued what was called a "Quiet Revolution" of economic and social development. The Union Nationale, which Lesage defeated, had been a classic patronage machine. It relied upon right-wing nationalist ideology and a cynical quid pro quo with Liberal governments in Ottawa for economic benefits in exchange for Quebecois political support for the federal Liberal candidates. Domestically, it relied upon a long-established clerical domination of social relations and state repression of civil liberties and of the rights of labor. Under these conditions, Anglophones, most of whom never bothered to learn French, occupied most positions of economic and administrative power.

The Liberals set about modernizing and secularizing Quebec, unleashing new Francophone forces. The success of the Quiet Revolution was assisted by the withdrawal of the Church, in response to criticism from Catholic intellectuals, from its intimate relation with the Union Nationale and its control of the trade union movement, and by the relaxation of the Church's claim to exclusive control of education and social welfare. In this development, the liberalizing influence of Pope John XXIII during the same time period is evident.

Provincial State Capitalism and Revolutionary Separatism

The provincial state actively promoted the transition from a largely agricultural to a more urban, industrial economy. Lesage's government professionalized and modernized the civil service and launched a wide range of projects, the most significant of which was creation of Hydro-Quebec, a huge multifaceted institution whose primary mandate was to promote economic and social development through hydroelectric projects. The company provided technical and managerial jobs for increasingly well-educated Quebecois. The government actively reformed and secularized education and launched new universities. In a period of economic prosperity, the provincial government became a major initiator of employment and infrastructural development.

When the modernization of Quebec began in the 1960s, government-controlled pension funds provided the first pool of capital for promoting bourgeois wealth creation.[1] These funds were used to establish the Caisse de Depot et Placement, whose mandate included investment in local government and hospital bond issues but also in share purchases of Quebec firms. By 1982, 15 percent of its holdings were shares in domestic companies, including Canada-based multinationals such as Alcan, Domtar Chemicals, and Consolidated Bathurst Paper, though there also were riskier purchases designed to consolidate and reorganize Quebec capital.

A second state agency designed to invest in the private sector was the Société Generale de Financement, established in 1962 with a mandate "to create Quebec industrial complexes and to participate in the management and financing of medium sized and large Quebec firms." These and other state agencies to alter the pattern of capital ownership and development were sponsored over the years by both Liberal and Parti Quebecois governments. If one includes the extensive development of cooperatives and credit unions in Quebec, which have also flourished under favorable government legislation and regulation, it is clear that the growth of the capitalist class—especially the Quebec bourgeoisie—has been a major task of the provincial state since the 1960s. The former leader of the Parti Quebecois, Jacques Parizeau, said, " . . . in Quebec, we must bring in the state. This is inevitable. It is what gives us an image of being more to the left. If we had, in Quebec, 25 Bombardier enterprises, and if we had very important banks, the situation would perhaps be different. We do not have large institutions, they must be created."[2]

But for the Quebec left, the growth of bourgeois nationalism was insufficient, since power still lay in the hands of the Anglo minority. The left began to agitate for a more radical attack on class and power distribution. In 1968, the Rassemblement pour l'Independence Nationale (RIN), the Mouvement Souveraineté-Association (MSA), the Ralliement National (RN), the small remnant of the right-wing Creditistes, and the Parti Socialiste du Quebec (PSQ) were brought together by René Lévesque, a renegade Liberal cabinet minister, to form the Parti Quebecois. The PQ sought political autonomy from the federal government but continued association with the rest of Canada for economic purposes, a goal it espouses to this day.

The revolutionary Front de Liberation du Quebec (FLQ) followed a different path: it operated in secret and adopted terrorist methods. In 1970, the FLQ abducted British Trade Commissioner J. R. Cross in Montreal and held him for ransom. Shortly thereafter a second cell of the group kidnapped and murdered Pierre Laporte, the provincial labor minister. This action prompted the Liberal provincial government of Robert Bourassa to request military intervention from the federal Liberal government of Prime Minister Pierre Trudeau, a Quebecker. The result was the October Crisis, in which the War Measures Act was proclaimed and the Canadian military occupied Quebec; civil law was suspended; offices were invaded and files expropriated; and thousands of political and labor activists were rounded up and held without charges. The few dozen members of the FLQ fled or were imprisoned and then reintegrated into Quebec life. But the memory of the extreme federal reaction continues to influence Quebec nationalist consciousness.

Class Change

Since 1960, the provincial state has played a decisive role in altering the class system as well as the relations of capital internally and externally. At the start of the Quiet Revolution, foreign investment, most of which was American, accounted for 41.8 percent of value-added production in the province; Anglo-Canadian capital owned 42.8 percent; Franco-Canadian capital claimed 15.4 percent. These proportions reflected the historic compromise whereby English-speaking Canadians controlled the Quebec economy and facilitated the same foreign investment pattern developed for the rest of Canada. The largest manufacturing and banking corporations—such as Alcan Aluminum, the Bank of Montreal, Sun Life Insurance—all regarded the rise of left-wing separatism as a threat and cast their weight with the Liberal federalists.

But Quebecois capitalists found considerable encouragement from both right and left separatists. Despite its initially strident separatist rhetoric, the Parti Quebecois, which contests only provincial elections, courted this newly developing class fraction and used the provincial government's legal, regulatory, and financial powers to promote its interests. In return, the Quebecois bourgeoisie (a class fraction concentrated in enterprises with 500 employees or less) and its closely related "new middle class" of educated and professional administrators became the main separatist activists.

Expansion of the state and its programs naturally created numerous and varied opportunities for the young, educated Quebecois who poured out of the new universities in the 1960s and 1970s. This army of employment seekers remain the shock troops of separatism, anticipating that independence will bring more opportunity. This is the class fraction that controls the Parti Quebecois and for whom its separatist strategy is designed.

The working class too was transformed by the activity of the state in the economy in the 1960s and after. Quebec was already an urban province by the time of the Quiet Revolution. Unlike the United States, the organized sector of the working class was mostly in conservative, Church-controlled, "confessional" unions. Expansion of the state vastly enlarged white-collar employment and altered the balance between white- and blue-collar unionism. Most of the new white-collar employees were organized in the Confederation des Syndicates National (CSR), originally Catholic but secular after 1960. Many of the unionized blue-collar workers were members of international unions and affiliated with the Canadian Labour Congress, represented in Quebec by the Federation de Travailleurs du Quebec (FTQ). That link entailed a bond with the federal New Democratic Party, which, as an Anglo social democratic party, was never accepted in Quebec. In 1975, the FTQ severed its NDP tie and today endorses the PQ. Teachers in Quebec, after secularization of the educational system, organized in the Centrale de l'Enseignement du Quebec (CEQ).

These trade unions were originally sympathetic to the left expression of nationalism espoused by the PQ in the 1970s, especially given the "concertation" strategy promoted by the government, a form of corporatism bringing together representatives of business, labor, and government to ameliorate class and industrial conflicts. This strategy was abandoned by the PQ in its second (1980s) administration as it moved away from separatism and adopted neo-liberal deficit control and stringency measures, including anti-labor legislation and actions. The focus of the PQ shifted exclusively to the national question.

Nationalism, the Constitution, and Canadian Politics

Prime Minister Pierre Trudeau was a stern enemy of Quebec nationalism from the time of his entry into federal politics in the 1960s. Throughout the 1970s, as he took control of the Liberal Party and government, he pushed the issues of bilingualism for Canada as a whole and the patriation of the constitution with an added charter of rights and freedoms. Such an agenda was intended to thwart the Quebec nationalists and demonstrate that Canada could be reformed to provide a secure and welcome home for the province and its culturally distinct population. So the federalist campaign of the Liberal government inevitably clashed with the left nationalist agenda of the Parti Quebecois, "Sovereignty Association"—a somewhat vague notion that Quebec could separate and yet not completely cut its economic ties with the rest of Canada. For some portion of the electorate, relief from Anglo Canada's domination and exploitation would only come with full and complete independence of Quebec as a separate nation-state. Others shared some of this sentiment but believed that Quebec was too small and weak to stand alone, or perceived important economic advantages to be had from association with Canada.

In 1980, in order to strengthen his position in the constitutional negotiations, Premier René Lévesque and his PQ government decided to hold a provincial referendum on the question of Sovereignty Association. The Trudeau federal government campaigned vigorously for a "no" vote, and the referendum lost. But this intervention by the federal Liberals and Trudeau, on top of the 1970 War Measures occupation, generated powerful political animosity among much of the French-speaking population of Quebec.

The mounting federal government campaign against the nationalist politics of Quebec and overt intervention reached a further crescendo in 1982 with the maneuvers employed to achieve agreement from a sufficient number of provinces to patriate the constitution of Canada. (Patriation refers to the legal transformation of the Canadian constitution, with British consent, from an act of the British Parliament to an act of the Canadian Parliament.) In the context of recurrent and intensifying conferences between provincial and federal governments, and in the aftermath of the referendum defeat, Trudeau promised that patriation of the constitution with a charter of rights would soon be achieved. At the crucial final four-day meeting of provincial first ministers in November 1981, a cabal of justice ministers from two provinces, together with Trudeau's Minister of Justice (and future prime minister) Jean Chrétien, hatched a compromise to include nine provinces and exclude Quebec.[3] The resulting constitutional package was never ratified by the Quebec National Assembly, but became the paramount law of the land for Canada. The means by which Quebec was excluded remains to this day a symbol for separatist leaders that Anglo-Canada rejects Quebec as either distinct or equal.

In 1985, the PQ itself was defeated by Robert Bourassa's Liberal Party. Bourassa, it should be remembered, was the man who as premier in 1970 had requested federal military intervention under the War Measures Act. His Liberal government remained federalist and supported the federal Progressive Conservative regime of Brian Mulroney, much as the right-wing Union Nationale of the 1940s and 1950s had supported federal governments. The out-of-office PQ went through an internal struggle that gave rise to a business nationalist strategy for total separation. Its adherents were and remain convinced that Quebec as an independent country can survive and prosper economically.

The move to the right by both the PQ and the Liberals during the 1980s is consistent with what happened in all other Canadian, indeed all advanced capitalist, political systems. What is unusual is that the election of the federal Progressive Conservative Party in 1984 depended entirely on the ability of Mulroney's first-time followers in Quebec to sweep away the perennial Liberal favorites. Some of this success came from provincial Liberals and Parti Quebecois followers angry at the Trudeau government for its campaign against the Quebec referendum and Trudeau's previous role in the 1970 October Crisis. Perhaps a stronger explanation was the role of Trudeau and his Quebec ministers in bringing the constitution to Canada in 1982 by excluding Quebec.

Yet because the structural requirements to serve the needs of the country as a whole are the same for any federal government, Tory members of Parliament from Quebec soon found themselves in conflict with the federal leadership. In 1990, most of the Quebec Conservatives broke away from the Mulroney government and formed a new party, the Bloc Quebecois (BQ), under the leadership of Lucien Bouchard. Bouchard was a close friend of Prime Minister Mulroney, but they found themselves at odds over Quebec separatism. The BQ is a nationalist formation contesting only federal elections on a separatist platform, attracting provincial right- and left-wing petty bourgeois and trade union nationalists, and drawing campaign support from the exclusively provincial Parti Quebecois.

Quebec's long record of ethnic nationalism leading to separatism poses a problem unlikely to be resolved in the short run. After the defeat of the referendum on Sovereignty Association in 1980, many thought that separatism was dead. René Lévesque, leader of the PQ at the time, had taken his message of separatism to Wall Street bankers, attempting to reassure them that their bonds were safe, but instead generated the greatest skepticism and some threats as to what the money markets might do. In the early 1990s, however, when the more technocratic PQ leader, Jacques Parizeau, made the same trip with the same message, he was met with yawns and complacent nods. American investors and bondholders were apparently indifferent to the outcome of this drama.

But English Canada is riven by conflicting reactions. In the 1990s, separatism, now a project of the Quebecois bourgeoisie, came back on the agenda, mainly because of the failure of Canada to amend the constitution so as to include Quebec. In 1987, Prime Minister Mulroney succeeded in reaching agreement with all the provincial premiers over amendments that would acknowledge the special character of Quebec. This so-called Meech Lake Agreement required unanimous approval of all provincial legislatures and the federal House of Commons. Newfoundland and Manitoba withheld their approval, and in 1990 the agreement failed. A second attempt in the fall of 1992, the Charlottetown Accord, was submitted to popular referendum, and it too was rejected. The Parti Quebecois and the Bloc Quebecois saw this as conclusive evidence that Quebec can never achieve a favorable amendment to the Constitution recognizing their uniqueness and distinct needs.

The 1993 federal election produced a bizarre result. Of Quebec's seventy-five federal seats the Bloc Quebecois won fifty-four, the Liberals nineteen, the Conservatives one, and an independent one. In the country at large both the Tories and NDP were swamped, but the right-wing populist Reform Party won fifty-two seats in the West. Ironically, then, the second largest party in the House of Commons and therefore the official, "loyal" opposition was the Bloc Quebecois, an avowed separatist organization committed to breaking the constitution, which Quebec has never endorsed. Furthermore, after 1993 the governing Liberals were once again led by a Quebecker and protégé of Pierre Trudeau, Jean Chrétien.

As the 1994 Quebec election drew near, BQ leader Lucien Bouchard traveled the country explaining to English Canadians that they must adjust to the inevitability of Quebec's separation. In the West reactions were hostile, both pro and con. Many, especially ultraright Reform Party supporters, said good riddance. Others wanted to know what the terms of separation would be, pointing out that in leaving, Quebec should take along only what it brought into Confederation—not including the vast northern territory allotted to the province in 1898 and 1912, which is occupied mainly by Indian

QUEBEC'S QUEST FOR NATIONHOOD

and Inuit peoples, few of whom speak French. Land claims remain unresolved. There are longstanding conflicts with the government of Quebec over the great hydroelectric complex under construction on James Bay. For these people, the prospect of government by Quebec without recourse to Ottawa is unattractive. Astride the New York state border, the Mohawk Indians pose another challenge to Quebec separatism, claiming their own independence from the authority of the jurisdictions in which they reside.

Perhaps a majority outside Quebec lament the prospect of separation; they worry that without Quebec, Canada will have less coherence and independence. The fear that English Canada will be absorbed by the United States is ever present. In May 1994, Bouchard alluded to this prospect, musing on the possibility of American territorial designs on British Columbia and Alberta if Quebec should secede. There is a nagging suspicion that English-speaking Canada is less culturally cohesive than Quebec. Yearly, as the country becomes more diverse, it tends more to an American-style "melting pot." Still, the visceral rejection of Americanism among Anglo-Canadians is real and powerful—fear of absorption remains tangible.

Another Separation Referendum

In anticipation of electoral victory in 1994, the Parti Quebecois published a detailed plan for separation titled *Quebec in a New World: The PQ's Plan for Sovereignty.* In it they declared that "the Quebec government will propose concluding an economic-association treaty or sectoral agreement that would maintain the Canadian economic space as it currently exists." The party was elected with a comfortable majority and directly announced its intention to hold a referendum on separation by the end of October 1995. PQ leaders were confident that Quebec could benefit from independent participation in NAFTA and the World Trade Organization. They expected the multilateral relations prescribed in those agreements—including a future common North American currency and financial harmonization—to diminish Quebec's historic dependence on the Canadian market.[4]

In the months leading up to the referendum vote, the federal government counseled calm and confidence in an assured negative result. During the early months of 1995 Prime Minister Chrétien repeated this advice to Canadians and issued dire warnings to Quebeckers about the financial, social, and political costs of a "yes" vote. Most big capitalists, both English and Quebecois, with all their international connections, opposed separation, seeing it as economically too risky and likely to disrupt their extensive connections with the rest of Canada. Some threatened to move their headquarters out of Montreal. In early October Premier Parizeau attacked the "financial elite for maintaining a federal system to protect their privileges at the expense of average taxpayers." He went on to say that "sovereignty is the only way to save Quebec from the kind of right-wing policies that Ontario has adopted lately."[5]

The new middle class and petty bourgeoisie in Quebec, however nationalistic, were not monolithic in their support for separation. The English-speaking population of 600,000 and the slightly smaller white ethnic minorities were generally federalist. These and the increasing third world immigrant population, bundled together under the title "allophones," were also generally but not uniformly federalist. Early opinion polls seemed to indicate skepticism over separation among the urban middle classes, especially in Montreal. But as the campaign ground on and the federal government failed to provide a positive reason for retaining the Canadian federation, the polls reflected a shift in attitude among the voters.

Organized labor was not significantly represented in the leadership of the PQ, which cannot be described as a friend of labor. Even so, both the trade unions and the left generally fell into support for the sovereignty project. They reasoned that the PQ is not a party of the big bourgeoisie, but a melange of social forces led by new middle class professionals. Labor and the left believed this composition left room for negotiation: after a "yes" vote the party could be persuaded or forced to bring in a radically left or socialist constitution, and there would be ample opportunity to establish collective rights, including collective bargaining, the right to strike, and the guarantee of social programs within such a constitution.[6]

As voting day approached in October 1995, the polls showed that public opinion had become equally divided. Since the federal government had still provided no alternative to separation, other supporters of unity began to take matters into their own hands. In "spontaneous" demonstration on the eve of the vote (inspired by Liberals and financed by federalist business and student organizations), English-speaking Canadians mounted a cavalcade to Montreal in which thousands of ordinary people expressed an emotional patriotic appeal to Quebeckers to stay in Confederation.

At the end, the vote was 49.5 percent against separation, 48.7 percent in favor: "No—by a Whisker," said the *Globe and Mail* on October 31. Premier Parizeau blamed the defeat on money and ethnics, and his outburst, broadcast to all of Canada, confirmed English-speakers' view that the Francophone separatists were fundamentally racist and ethnic nationalists.

In the course of the campaign, important tactical differences had developed between Parizeau, the PQ leader who was nominally in charge, and the politically popular Bouchard, leader of the federal Bloc Quebecois. Although Bouchard officially took a deferential back seat, Parizeau, a technocrat turned politician, enjoyed much less popular support and was thus persuaded to designate Bouchard as negotiator for Quebec with the federal government should the referendum be won by the separatists. After the defeat and Parizeau's offensive statement, he was forced to withdraw as leader. In 1996, the party chose Bouchard (who then resigned as Bloc leader).

Bouchard immediately set to work to heal differences with big business and with the linguistic and ethnic minorities, setting the issue of another referendum on the back burner. His provincial administration aimed at repairing the economy, creating jobs, and reducing the budget deficit. Nevertheless, he remains verbally committed to a further vote on separation. For their part, the federal Liberals have been stalled over a strategy to anticipate another referendum. They claim to be developing an inviting Plan A and an aggressively defensive Plan B, the one a soft and the other a hard approach. Thus far only the latter has been revealed in any detail. By encouraging the indigenous peoples in their declaration that if the Quebecois can declare independence, so can they, it addresses the sovereigntists' vulnerability to charges of ethnic chauvinism. Plan B also challenges the borders of an independent Quebec, queries the share of the federal debt to which an independent Quebec would be liable, and asks who has the right to define a future referendum question and whether independent Quebeckers would be allowed to retain Canadian citizenship. In 1997, a further hard-line step was taken by launching a request to the Supreme Court to rule on whether and under what conditions a declaration of independence would be lawful.

All these reactive tactics ascribed to Plan B highlight the absence of any constructive proposals for continuing Confederation under Plan A. Actually, the scant strategy proposed for national unity is internally and historically counterproductive of unity. Despite the evident importance to Canada of the central state and of nationwide, shared-cost social programs, the main agenda of the federal government in the 1990s has been to devolve various social programs to the provinces. Because Quebec has insisted on greater power to govern itself, because the neoliberal business agenda demands a reduction in government size and function, and because what is fair and proper for one province must be for all, Plan A proposes renunciation of federal powers of spending and regulating. Specifically Ottawa has turned over to the provinces (especially Quebec) labor-market training authority. Without adequate funding, this authority will fall unevenly on the provinces in proportion to their different economic capabilities. More profoundly, ordinary people in Quebec will find no difficulty in repudiating the federal government if it ceases to have functions important to them.

Jean Chrétien has been discredited by his miscalculation of how close the referendum vote might be, which was followed by the widespread realization that another vote would surely win. Subsequently, he has supplied so little imagination and leadership that the Business Council on National Issues has itself taken the initiative to assemble a conference of political, administrative, and academic leaders to develop and put before Quebec a national unity plan acceptable to the business community of Canada as a whole. Other evidence of broader public anxiety over the failure of federal leadership includes initiatives by some left intellectuals to generate an alternative Plan C. According to one version of this, Canadians would be urged to understand that Canada as a country would not dissolve and collapse into the United States if Quebec were to separate, that Quebec is not what makes the Canadian state necessary or possible. The proposal includes the demand to address the deficiencies of Anglo-Canadian democracy and the need for a genuinely popular, wholly reconstructed constitution. In this perspective the Quebec crisis offers the opportunity to address the inadequacies of the overall Canadian power system.

Just how volatile and unending the national unity issue is became evident again in the 1997 federal election. The Liberals—far ahead in advanced polls, enjoying a comfortable majority in Parliament, basking in the success of their deficit-cutting strategy and evidence of growth in the economy—anticipated a quiet and uncontentious campaign. But Preston Manning, the leader of the Reform Party, launched a bitter attack against all federalist parties that might want to ameliorate the national conflict by adopting constitutional language acknowledging Quebec's special status. The Liberal lead dwindled, leaving Chrétien with a bare majority and facing Reform—representing only western Canadian constituencies—as the official opposition, determined to oppose concessions to Quebec.

The "French fact," more precisely the Quebec fact, has played a continuing role in sustaining the structure of power in Canada. As ancient Athenian rulers discovered, foreign enemies and the threat of conflict can be useful in preserving the rule of an individual or regime. The Soviet Union and communism played such a role in the United States for forty-four years after the Second World War. Since Confederation the perpetually unresolved problem of Quebec's status has provided the drama of threat and relief between provincial and federal Canadian governments and between the two dominant political parties.

In Canadian public life, the importance of the Quebec issue has only increased. Despite the mortal attack by financial capital against the entire structure of Canadian social programs, and the eclipse of economic autonomy, the single most important domestic concern is the prospect that sovereigntists may win a Quebec referendum and separate the country constitutionally. It is in this sense that the Quebec issue functions as an internal "enemy," polarizing the rest of the population between right-wing racists and bigots who want an end to "special pleading," and Canadian moderates seeking to accommodate Quebec's legitimate demands. Bound up in a seemingly perpetual constitutional crisis, neither pole can address the overriding issues of imperialism and class conflict for either a united Canada or a separate Quebec.

Chapter 6

The State and Its Record

Canadian voters and politicians take it as natural that the state will be invoked to solve problems that individuals, even corporate individuals, will not or cannot. Too often, of course, business taps the public purse, regulatory capability, or diplomatic assistance for private benefit. From its colonial origin, for example, the Canadian state has played a key role in fostering international trade. But because it is broadly legitimate in Canadian political culture to invoke state assistance for collective purposes, the lower social classes, minority nationalities, and people's organizations have also routinely demanded and achieved governmental patronage. This active state has been a defining feature of Canadian experience, especially since the Second World War, when the social safety net of pensions, welfare system, health system, and similar social components was installed and extended to the whole country. Canada relies heavily upon government to initiate and manage development, to ameliorate class and national conflict, to achieve a measure of social harmony.

By contrast, ever since the Revolution, Americans have regarded the federal government with suspicion, as a real or potential threat to their individual rights. Indeed, there was not even broad support for George Washington and the Continental Army, and the Articles of Confederation designed a central government so weak it could not marshal the material means to fight the war. From the beginning, fear of too much power in government has been characteristic of U.S. public life. That theme is actively projected by large and small business in objection to spending on the lower classes—but not on subsidy of the military and business. The hostility to government and politics permeates all classes, encourages right-wing populism, and—with the exception of the

Rooseveltian New Deal—dissuades even honest and sincere politicians from using government to launch serious reform initiatives.

The historian Tom Naylor said, "Canada in its conception was the most centralized of all the classical federations of the world, with stronger federal control than the U.S., Australia or Switzerland."[1] All important monetary, financial, and trade power was located in the federal government, and Canada's constitution granted residual powers to the federal state (those unspecified powers that allow a government to adapt to changing historical circumstances beyond what could be envisaged in enumerated powers). In the U.S. Constitution, which reflected the prior existence and decisive role of the individual colonies in constructing it, residual powers were retained by the states and thereby the local dominant class interests. In the twentieth century, however, this has been reversed for all intents and purposes by locating income-taxing power in Washington, by mobilization for two world wars, and by the Depression-era collapse of the fiscal integrity of individual states.

In another indication of the Canadian intention to create a powerful central state, the federal government was empowered to veto provincial legislation. Further, members of its Senate were not elected but appointed for life, to protect against the possibility that the elected House of Commons might fall into the hands of "dangerous" classes. The provinces were awarded responsibility for local education, health, municipal institutions, incorporations, marriages, and property and civil rights.

The Anglo-Canadian and British financial interests for whom this state was established had reason to be pleased with its performance. New territories were soon acquired by voluntary recruitment and purchase. In the 1870s, Prince Edward Island in the East, and Rupert's Land and British Columbia in the West were added to the dominion.

The original intention of the founding fathers to create a strong central state with powers to shape the new nation did not go unchallenged. Local interests in the provinces early sought to use their own governments to resist invasion by those narrow financial and commercial powers which controlled the federal state. In nineteenth century America, a similar conflict between the states and federal government occurred. The U.S. Supreme Court devoted much attention to the scope of the Constitution's commerce clause, which frequently entailed awarding privileges and immunities to local, as opposed to national, economic interests. In Canada, however, final appeal rested not in a domestic Supreme Court but in the Judicial Committee of the Privy Council in London. These councilors were used to a unitary (as opposed to a federal) system with a sovereign parliament and no written constitution. Their literal reading of the British North America Act curtailed federal powers to the advantage of the provinces, thus creating stronger local power bases than the founding fathers had intended. In a series of decisions at the end of the nineteenth and beginning of the twentieth century, they gave very wide interpretation to the constitutional meaning of property and civil rights in the provinces, restricted the federal power over trade and commerce, and relegated the "peace order and good government" concept (Canada's elastic constitutional clause, expanding the limited powers of the federal government) to wartime emergency.

This decentralization of Canadian state power worked to the advantage of U.S. capital as it began to establish itself in Canada after the turn of the twentieth century. The British North America Act located regulation of industrial relations in the provinces, which were eager to attract foreign investment and pleased to oblige with minimal regulatory and tax impediments, competing with one another to offer U.S. investors favorable treatment.

Labor-management relations in Canada during the early decades of this century were every bit as turbulent and violent as in the United States, particularly in the western timber and mining industries. The federal state regularly provided Dominion police and militia to battle and imprison workers in British Columbia, Alberta, and Saskatchewan. One of the key figures in developing early state strategy to control strikes was William Lyon Mackenzie King, who served as an adviser to John D. Rockefeller in the aftermath of "Bloody Ludlow," the 1914 massacre in Colorado that ended a strike in Rockefeller's coal mines.[2] King's decades-long career as civil servant and politician was most important in developing a ruling strategy for containing and ameliorating class conflict. As minister of labor, leader of the Liberal Party, and prime minister, he presided over 1920s prosperity, the second half of the Great Depression, mobilization for the Second World War, and postwar demobilization. His ideological heirs remained in virtually uninterrupted command of the Canadian state until 1984.

Such continuity of control by a single party and a single man did much to consolidate the power and function of the central state. This was particularly the case in the response to the Depression. Like the individual American states, the Canadian provinces were fiscally incapable of coping with the magnitude of their responsibilities for infrastructure, social services, and alleviation of poverty. When the Depression began, Prime Minister Richard B. Bennett, a Conservative businessman from Alberta, initially responded to the collapse much as did Stanley Baldwin in England and Herbert Hoover in the United States: allowing the economy to take its ruinous course and repressing workers who took collective action.

For example, unemployed single men in Canadian cities were rounded up and shipped off to secluded camps in the undeveloped interior, where they worked on civil engineering projects under military discipline. In 1935, a small army of these young men started a cross-country trek from British Columbia by rail to Ottawa to demand state action for real jobs.[3] In panic, the Conservative government ordered them stopped by the Royal Canadian Mounted Police (RCMP). In the middle of the prairies a battle ensued at Regina, and the trek was halted. Somewhat chastened, Prime Minister Bennett looked south to Roosevelt's New Deal for reforms to ease the economic crisis, but his efforts were overruled by a conservative Supreme Court, and Bennett was soon defeated.

Nevertheless, evidence that the provinces did not have the resources to meet major crises gave rise in 1937 to the Royal Commission on Dominion-Provincial Relations. From this came a system of equalization based on a communitarian notion of common interest and common good: the federal and provincial governments would redistribute tax revenues to overcome the uneven economic and social development of the nation. That principle of equalization provided the foundation for a system of social programs to supplement the working wage, which was gradually expanded throughout three and a half decades after the Second World War.

In 1944, nearly ten years after passage of the National Labor Relations Act in the United States, the Canadian federal government legalized collective bargaining. At the end of the war, the state set about developing a comprehensive social welfare system based upon the principle of universal coverage for all Canadians in all provinces. During the postwar boom, the federal and provincial states benefited from expanding budgets, moderate but acceptable inflation, relative industrial peace, and in general the kind of Keynesian redistribution experienced by most advanced capitalist countries. In international relations, the military was recruited into the Korean War but not on a scale that required the economic remobilization that occurred in the United States.

In 1949, the Canadian Parliament passed legislation discontinuing judicial appeals to the House of Lords, making the Canadian Supreme Court the final court of appeal. This seemingly belated act of autonomy began a process that would result in the final legal separation of Canada from Britain: the patriation of the Canadian constitution in 1982 and the adoption of a Charter of Rights and Freedoms. At that point the court acquired ultimate powers of interpretation and adjudication between provincial and federal aspects of the state, and since then the Canadian judiciary has adopted a more active role in review of legislation and regulatory proceedings, shedding the judicial restraint associated with traditions of parliamentary sovereignty and moving toward a U.S.-style legalization of politics.[4] As in the entire history of the United States, the unelected Supreme Court now exerts its predominantly conservative ideological influence in Canadian politics.

In the 1970s, the prosperity of the immediate postwar years turned to economic stagnation and double-digit inflation. The federal Liberal government, which had become the state party wielding the tool of Keynesianism, could no longer expect to stimulate economic growth with inflationary fiscal policies. Instead, to stem the soaring inflation, it introduced mandatory wage and price controls, which under the circumstances effectively put an end to negotiated wage increases without having much effect on prices. It also imposed an onerous system of recordkeeping on businesses, which were now beginning to listen to the siren songs of deregulation from the neoliberals amongst them.

War between Arabs and Israel in 1973 resulted in Arab states taking control of their oil production, with worldwide inflationary results: an immediate threefold increase in the price of crude oil was transmitted by the international industry to world production and marketing, creating windfall profits for companies but no commensurate increases for the governments who were major consumers of oil and gas. Capitalist governments generally accepted this overnight price inflation as an "act of God" about which little could be done but to accept market price as an inducement to curtail oil use. In contrast, the social democratic NDP government of Saskatchewan in 1974 amended provincial tax schedules to use its power to capture some of the profits. The oil industry, supported by the federal government, protested this provincial state action to the Supreme Court, arguing that an export tax violated the constitutional division of powers which assigns indirect taxation exclusively to the federal government. The provincial action was overruled. The limits of "socialism in one province" were reaffirmed.

Nevertheless, the oil price crisis in the context of mounting inflation did demand federal government action. From the earliest years of the modern Canadian state, it has been normal to create crown corporations to achieve national and provincial objectives. From railroads, canals, airlines, ports, and airports to pharmaceuticals, broadcasting, and grain marketing, government-owned production and service companies have been more common in Canada than in any other advanced capitalist country except France. Hence, in 1975, the Liberals, influenced by the government minority NDP, established Petro-Canada as a state-owned oil company initially limited to fostering greater exploration than private industry was willing to undertake. Petro-Canada was also intended to provide "a window on the industry," retain profits in Canada, train more Canadian oil technicians, and sponsor research.

In a further action, the Liberal government in 1981 passed the National Energy Program (NEP). The announced objective was greater energy self-sufficiency, conservation, nation-building, and Canadianization. The western oil industry and provincial governments protested that the real intention was to perpetuate Liberal Party hegemony in central Canadian economies at the expense of the West.

In an economic environment of stagflation, state interventions in the economy, loaded with East-versus-West political significance, contributed to a migration of capitalists away from the Trudeau Liberal Party's Keynesian strategies. Manipulating the money supply by expanding and contracting interest rates increasingly came to be the preferred method of government influence in the economy. The Bank of Canada, substantially independent of direct government influence, sets official interest rates weekly, and in doing so pays extreme attention to what the U.S. Federal Reserve Board is doing and what Wall Street and European money markets are saying. (This extroverted orientation contrasts sharply with the approach of the Federal Reserve Board, which pays greatest attention to what is required to prod or restrain the U.S. economy.)

Through these monetarist policies, the traditional interventionism of the Canadian state has been turned around. At election time in 1984, the Progressive Conservative Party (PC) gave no indication of the direction it would ultimately take. Its new leader, Brian Mulroney, a perfectly bilingual

Tory from Quebec with an attractive, liberal-sounding image, vowed to restore harmony between the provincial and federal governments and to continue the system of equalization and social programs but to remove the intrusive hand of the federal state from the economy. The Liberals were defeated resoundingly, most especially in Quebec—their political stronghold for decades—and in the West.

The United States in 1984 had already experienced nearly four years of Ronald Reagan, whose economic and governing strategy was apparent: international bellicosity, domestic union-busting, and rewards for the wealthy at the cost of declining living standards for most. Next to that of Reagan and Margaret Thatcher, Mulroney's conservatism seemed mild and inoffensive at first. But almost from the start, members of his government were engaged in a variety of self-aggrandizing scandals. An attempt to cut old-age pensions, defeated by a massive demonstration of outraged senior citizens, hinted of neoliberal moves to come. A Royal Commission, set up under the leadership of a former Liberal finance minister to inquire into Canada's economic strategy, recommended that Canada should seek a free-trade agreement with the United States. Simultaneously, the PC government began an aggressive campaign to sell off crown corporations, abolish the National Energy Program, convert its Investment Review Agency into a body to promote foreign investment, and implant the notion that government debt and deficit were the primary issues of public policy in Canada. "Downsizing" of the state, deregulation, and degradation of social programs became the strategy of government from 1984 to 1993. Nor was it restricted to the federal state; provincial governments of all political stripes, attempting to satisfy the demands of international financial lenders, especially Wall Street, adopted neoliberal conventional wisdom during the same time period.

In 1993, a Liberal government was elected on a platform of job creation based upon renewal of the public works infrastructure, a program promising to correct the policies of the previous Conservative regime. The new government canceled the planned sale of the Toronto Airport to a private consortium; it stepped in to support East Coast fishermen, whose industry had collapsed as a result of overfishing; it canceled a lavish Defense Department helicopter purchase contract and cut deeply into military spending, to the detriment of industries and political constituencies long dependent on Cold War subsidization.

In the newly emerging context of international economic restructuring, however, with intense pressures being exerted to harmonize capitalist state fiscal and monetary strategies, the Liberal government soon met intensified pressure from international money markets and Wall Street bondholders. The first evidence was a run on the Canadian dollar in the first week of April 1994. Between early February (when the U.S. Federal Reserve Board began raising its interest rates) and early April, the Canadian dollar lost 3 percent of its value against the U.S. dollar, a decline of four cents. In February, the Bank of Canada put $1.7 billion worth of currency reserves, 15 percent of its holdings, into shoring up the dollar. Canadian financial interpreters of these developments blamed the accumulated budgetary debt, which stood at more than 70 percent of Gross Domestic Product, and the deficit. The Federal Reserve Board was ignored when it decided to increase interest rates when Canada and other Western economies were just emerging from a protracted recession; nothing could be done about it short of cutting Canada loose from U.S. interest rates. There followed a declaration of resolve by the finance minister to bring down the federal budget deficit from $45 billion to $25 billion in three years "come hell or high water." Toughness of resolve was then trumpeted to Canada and the international market at the expense of all other programs.

A vivid example of the way in which money market demands preempt domestic governmental agendas is the fate of a review of social program delivery. The minister of human resources (social welfare) had previously announced plans for a major review of the entire system of social services—but in November 1995 this project, which had already been deliberated by provincial governments and public groups for more than a year, was shelved in favor of all-out budget retrenchment. The finance minister made clear that he intended to terminate the existing federal-provincial funding procedures in favor of "bloc grants" to the provinces, albeit in lower amounts than in the past. Such a step would effectively remove the ability to enforce normative standards by federal funding, since each provincial administration could decide for itself how funds would be spent. Throughout the 1980s the federal government had incrementally turned back to the provinces responsibility for the provision of health, welfare, and education programs. Now the funding would be reduced by $7 billion, and the bloc funds delivered with freedom for the provinces to spend as they see fit. At the end of March 1996 Ottawa abandoned the Canada Assistance Plan—for thirty years the centerpiece of the shared-cost social safety net—turned welfare over entirely to the individual provinces. There can be no doubt that this arrangement will lead to a patchwork of reduced standards of service delivery while making it more difficult for provinces with smaller revenue bases to balance their own budgets. It will also make them more independently responsible to the bond-trading financiers of Wall Street and Toronto's Bay Street.

Dismantling the Canadian state structure that stood for more than fifty years on the Keynesian model is in line with U.S. and International Monetary Fund (IMF) plans. Some 40 percent of Canada's public debt is held by foreign financial institutions, 25 percent by Japan. In mid-February 1995, the international credit rating firm Moody's Investors Service, knowing that the Canadian budget would be introduced at the end of the month, announced it was putting Canada on a credit watch. This statement was front-page news for the better part of a week, prompting repeated assurances from Finance Minister Paul Martin.

The pressure worked. At the end of February the finance minister announced a draconian budget, slashing $13.6 billion over two years—the largest two-year reduction ever. No aspect of government activity was spared deep cuts. Targeted for dismissal were 45,000 government workers, 14 percent of the federal civil service. Defense spending was cut 14 percent, to $9.9 billion. Transfer payments to provinces for equalization in social programs, including education, were cut $5.3 billion. Ontario and Quebec were forced to absorb 71 percent of the loss though they account for only 63 percent of the country's population. Plans were announced to privatize Canadian National Railway, Petro-Canada, numerous airports, and the country's air navigation system. A cut in funding for the Canadian Broadcasting Corporation of $350 million over three years was expected to put an end to the CBC's role as the public broadcaster. Prairie farmers lost one of their historic benefits of this century, the Crow Rate, or rail transportation subsidy for grain. Quebec and Ontario milk producers lost their dairy subsidies.

Some portion of this strategy was directed at satisfying Quebec's traditional demand for greater governmental autonomy prior to its upcoming sovereignty referendum. Since the 1960s, all Quebec governments have sought and often achieved greater independence than other provinces enjoy in the establishment of programs, standards, and management of their own revenues and expenditures. Some Anglo provinces applauded the decentralization of fiscal authority as well, but most, especially those headed by NDP governments, have been sharply critical of the likely loss of federal governing authority. Canada's national newspaper, the *Globe and Mail,* commented, "Mr. Martin's budget [marks] a radical rolling back of the state for a government that has spent the past five decades extending its reach into all manner of activities."[5] Yet to be attacked is the $20 billion Canada Pension Plan, which the finance minister vows to "examine," a process begun in the summer of 1996.

The first motive of the federal Liberal government in reversing the postwar priority on a strong central government was conformity to the new international standards of reorganizing capital. A second motive was internal: a desire of the federal treasury to escape the automatic requirement to finance provincial budgetary shortfalls. Provincial equalization payments have been central to the Canadian standard of living since the Second World War, taxes from "have" provinces being redistributed to "have not" provinces to compensate spending in social programs so that all Canadians could expect a comparable standard of services regardless of where they live. During a period of recession such as that of the 1990s, more provinces have been in distress than have been prosperous, and according to existing agreements the shortfall must be made up by the federal treasury. It is the unilateral termination of this arrangement that the finance minister intends, so that when the next major downturn occurs in the economy, local governments and the individuals they are supposed to serve shall be forced to carry the burden.

As Canada has some characteristics of a third world colony, it is logical that IMF restructuring policies and core financial institutions should attack and destroy the mechanisms of self-protection that have been built to secure some degree of autonomy: the state, social programs, cultural institutions. The 1995 Canadian federal budget, considered as a strategy document, reveals how purposeful Wall Street and the U.S. trade commissioner are in this objective. Once again, their demands elicited compliant responses from Canadian rulers. Speaking in 1974 of the effects of capital internationalization on sovereign states, Nicos Poulantzas said, "[t]hese states themselves take charge of the interest of the dominant imperialist capital in its development within the 'national' social formation . . . in its complex relation of internationalization to the domestic bourgeoisies."[6] Leo Panitch observes, "Transnational capital's interpenetration with domestic bourgeoisies may have rendered the notion of a national bourgeoisie increasingly arcane. . . ."[7] Applying this reasoning to the eager embrace by the Canadian ruling class of Free Trade and NAFTA, Panitch continues:

> *This is not something imposed on the Canadian and Mexican states by American capital and state as external. . . . rather it reflects the role adopted by the Mexican and Canadian states in representing the interests of their bourgeoisies and bureaucracies as these are already penetrated by American capital and administration.*[8]

Thus, in the 1990s, the state in Canada, much as in all capitalist countries, is administered according to conservative, monetarist principles. The achieved levels of social programs during the past forty-five years are being eroded, but the forms remain. It is not yet clear how profound this finance-induced change of strategy in the role of the state will be. The Canadian state cannot abandon its interventionist and regulatory role without endangering the independent existence of Canada. The social and economic role of the Canadian state, despite the rhetoric of neoliberalism, was forced upon successive Liberal governments by popular demands arising from class and national conflicts, and it resulted in a different political environment from that of the United States.

Because of that shaping role of popular demand, debate tends to focus on national issues and how they are to be solved for the sake of Canadian identity and unity. In the 1997 federal election campaign, for example, the governing Liberals took pride in having brought the budget deficit virtually to an end, then turned to promises of restoring spending to cherished social programs hard hit in the drive to regain fiscal probity. Popular demand also tends to force clarity of stance by politicians and visibility in respect to those issues; public awareness of and participation in debate over issues is relatively high. Certainly, since the increased activity of people's organizations, rulers have been forced to adopt inclusive public forums, even referendums, to deal with contentious constitutional and legislative issues.

Canadian politics and society are less spontaneous, explosive, and rebellious than U.S. politics and society, reflecting different attitudes toward and experience with state power. The dominant position of the state coincides with a long tradition of conservative, elitist, and bureaucratic rule so long as the limiting formalities of parliamentary democracy are observed. Nevertheless, organized public pressure has often been able to force a strong, actively intervening state to serve the interests of subordinate classes. That is evident in the major political struggles of past and recent history.

Chapter 7

Political Struggles in Canada

Guerrilla war, general strikes, and mass demonstrations: these dramatic, but in Canada uncommon, manifestations remind us of the class differences in society and the unquenchable urge of those at the bottom for a more just arrangement.

Politics, in contrast, is normally represented as something of interest only to an elite, a striving between a special few who have narrow personal gain at stake. But the truth is that whether we are aware of it or not, politics is one of the most important and pervasive expressions of class conflict, intruding on daily life and shaping values, attitudes, and behavior.

The United States is preeminent among liberal democratic nations in the absence from active electoral participation of such a large proportion of its population and in the lack of any political party of the lower classes. Since the Democratic and Republican parties, which enjoy a monopoly over formal politics, belong to different fractions of capital, it is not surprising that politics is widely discredited among the general population as something alien that "they" do.

"They," of course, are the owners of capital and their administrative, professional, and academic allies and servants. Politics in the United States has become primarily an arena of contention between parts of the same or closely related classes; other classes are maneuvered to the margins of civic life, though they must continually be recruited or pacified to endorse the decisions, judgments, and actions of the Democratic or Republican leaders. Since the 1950s, an unusually high proportion of the American public has been a substantially passive audience for formal and informal political actors.

Canada's Dominant Parties

In Canada, likewise, two political parties are dominant: Conservatives and Liberals have ruled at the federal level throughout 130 years of independence. What is different is that since the 1930s there have been significant additional parties representing and controlled by dissident social groups. These have variously expressed right and left populism, social democracy and reaction, and have represented the interests of farmers, workers, and small business.

As in the United States, the two dominant parties in Canada are controlled by different fractions of capital and are typically funded on a shifting pattern of 60 percent for one and 40 percent for the other. Also as in the United States, they can be successful only if they can win the votes of those with little or no capital: fishermen, farmers, middle managers, workers, the unemployed, women, youth, and the aged. In the absence of a working class political consciousness highly developed over many generations, the Liberal Party has been continually successful in competing with the New Democratic Party (NDP), its major rival for support from the subordinate classes. The Conservative (now Progressive Conservative)[1] Party has normally been successful in winning the support of right-wing populists and conservative small capitalists who are also the target of such regional parties of the right as Social Credit, Reform, and Bloc Quebecois. The dominant parties therefore play the same role in obscuring class issues as do the U.S. Democrats and Republicans.

In the United States, the continuous process of containing subordinate class demands for meaningful politics has led to massive voter withdrawal and cynicism. This withdrawal, quietly encouraged by both Republicans and Democrats, contrasts with high levels of political participation by the largely white middle and owning classes who have a significant political stake in property protection. The same narrowing of the electorate is not part of Canadian political strategy. Federal electoral turnout is normally in the range of 65 to 75 percent of eligible voters, in contrast to U.S. federal elections which seldom attract as much as 55 percent. What is remarkable is that the small class of capitalists in Canada, amounting to no more that 1 percent of the population, can divide its forces between two political parties, recruit electoral support from the middle and lower classes, and still retain a high level of popular participation in the political process. This amounts to popular endorsement of class rule, and it requires explanation.

One simple explanation is that the Canadian political system makes it relatively easy to vote: Canadian voters are enumerated in their homes by the state before every election, whereas Americans must register with a government office and request the right to vote. Further, civic consciousness remains relatively high in Canada, where voters have not resigned themselves to sullen rejection of the formal political process as so many Americans have. Patterns of voluntary social participation remain high in Canada. Community and people's organizations flourish, and polls and open-line programs indicate a vigorous civic life.

Social Movements as Political Actors

Among the most fundamental and enduring social movements that have shaped the Canadian experience and to some extent continue to influence public life and personal behavior is the cooperative movement. For the first four or five decades of the twentieth century, farming and fishing communities relied upon cooperatives for retail supplies, markets for their products, and banks for loans. In western Canada, cooperatives took on significance similar to their role in Britain and Scandinavia in the early part of this century. The movement was also important in the Maritimes during the 1930s and in Quebec after 1960. In 1935 a group of Saskatchewan farmers pooled sufficient capital to build an oil refinery that thrives to this day.

Most significant of these self-help institutions was the cooperative pooling of grain in Manitoba, Saskatchewan, and Alberta. Today these Wheat Pools are among the largest accumulations of native Canadian capital; in 1992 the Saskatchewan Wheat Pool posted profits of $40 million. In contrast to such American giants as Cargill, Bunge, and Continental, they did not become transnational imperialist corporations; instead, they forced the federal government in the 1930s to create the Canadian Wheat Board to act as an international seller of all Canadian grains. Nevertheless, the pressures of "globalization" have also reached the Pools. In 1996, in order to gain access to the international investment market, the Saskatchewan Wheat Pool—largest of the agricultural cooperatives, with assets of $1.3 billion and 1995 consolidated revenues of $3.9 billion—became a share-offering company on the Toronto Stock Exchange. At the same time, the existence of the Canadian Wheat Board is under mounting attack by U.S. and domestic opponents, who regard it as a restraint on free trade.

In earlier years, the cooperative movement was the most important vehicle for mobilizing people at the grassroots level for all manner of community development purposes. Some parts of the movement generated a searching critique of capitalism. Cooperatives, together with the social gospel, a progressive movement in the Protestant church, formed an important strand of socialist politics in Canada. But most cooperatives remained populist, with all the grievances of small capital confronting large capital (typically identified with Toronto, Montreal, and New York). When the Co-operative Commonwealth Federation was formed, it was considered simply a political arm of the cooperative movement.

In Europe, trade unions were active in developing their own cooperatives. In Canada, on the contrary, as the most successful co-ops became large and bureaucratized, overt labor-management conflict developed. Workers, previously considered part of "the co-op family," increasingly organized into trade unions, confronting uncomprehending co-op owners and business-school-trained managers. Since the 1950s, some of the resulting strikes have been bitter and protracted. This conflict led to attenuation between the co-op movement and the CCF, especially when it transformed itself into the NDP in 1961. Traditional cooperatives are no longer found among the popular organizations that are contesting the dominant business agenda. The most vital expressions of cooperativism today exist among the weak and ill-served. The cooperatives that continue to mobilize volunteers and educate them in self-help are the marginal initiatives of daycare providers, community health services, battered women and pregnancy counseling, indigenous communities, immigrant aid, and solidarity organizations.

Reactionary Reform

At the other end of the Canadian political spectrum, right-wing populism and reaction have been a continuous force, though until recently less significant than that represented by social democracy. Populism has its home in rural communities and petty bourgeois occupations, small business, and conservative Christianity. In 1935, the Evangelical minister William Eberhart, taking up the vague Social Credit economic philosophy of Major C. H. Douglas of Britain, led a crusade in reaction against the tired United Farmers of Alberta government, sweeping it into history and launching three decades of right-wing populist rule in that province. Although the Social Credit party had its base in the agricultural and ranching population, it was the discovery of oil in the 1940s that assured its continued reelection in the province, even as the rural population dwindled. As a result of oil and gas revenues, Alberta to this day is the bastion of ideological reaction in Canada. For example, successive right-wing governments have rejected imposition of a sales tax despite the debt and deficit that they say necessitates cutting the health care budget by 20 percent, selling to private medical groups the hospitals they have forced to close, and generally introducing a model reflecting the U.S. health industry.

A subsequent Social Credit party without the economic metaphysic was formed in British Columbia, where it governed for most of forty years until 1991. In Quebec, a Creditiste party existed briefly and unsuccessfully in the 1960s and 1970s. With these provincial bases, Social Credit was able to form a federal party and to elect members to Parliament between 1935 and 1979, reaching a high of thirty seats in 1962. But the movement could never break out of its regional and declining agrarian base to constitute a significant threat to its ideological ally, the Progressive Conservatives. That party, in 1958, chose western right-wing populist John Diefenbaker as its leader and achieved one of the great landslide electoral victories of the century. Diefenbaker was prime minister when John F. Kennedy was U.S. president. Their relationship was prickly, and when under the provisions of NORAD the Canadian military was summarily mobilized during the Cuban missile crisis without prior consultation with Diefenbaker, the repercussions split the Conservative cabinet and contributed to the downfall of the government. (Most in the United States are unaware that their rulers' making and breaking of foreign governments occurs with such "friends" as Canada, not simply distant enemies such as Allende's Chile or Sandinista Nicaragua.)

Like the U.S. West, western Canada remains a seedbed of voter resentment and political reaction among those who perceive discrimination against their interests by the wealthy and populous East. In 1987, Preston Manning, son of the last leader of Alberta's Social Credit government, launched a new Reform Party to contest only federal elections. Reform combines populist rhetoric and right-wing big business ambitions, evoked by Manning with a folksy demagoguery similar to that of Newt Gingrich and Ross Perot in the United States. (In March 1995, Manning, who resembles Perot, was crowned by the Washington press corps "Newt of the North.") Support for Reform has been built on cynicism and anger among a class of Canadians being squeezed by the consequences of global economic restructuring and the relative inability or unwillingness of the major political parties to relieve their distress.

Victories for capitalist restructuring under conditions of stagnation and unemployment have unleashed disturbing forces which threaten Canada's tradition of social solidarity. Tension over third world immigration, prolonged high unemployment, destruction of the independent commodity producer, the increasing militancy of class, gender, and national fractions long denied equal membership in public life, and the loss of patience on both sides of the Quebec national question are all elements in the growth of an ugly right-wing reaction.

At the extreme right, the Heritage Front, like the U.S. Aryan Nation, is a violent formation opposed to nonwhite immigrants, indigenous peoples, and Jews. It was preceded by pro-Nazi organizations that arose in Quebec, Saskatchewan, and elsewhere during the 1930s and even during the war. The Ku Klux Klan, as well, was active on the prairies in the 1920s and 1930s and at present still operates in the large cities. Social Credit and the Progressive Conservatives have always attracted reactionary and racist members. In the 1980s and 1990s, manifestations of anti-Semitism, racism, and militant anti-abortion activism all surfaced violently. Thus far the extent and intensity of these expressions is far less severe than in the United States. One of the holdouts in the 1996 showdown between federal marshals and Freemen militia in Montana was a former Calgary police officer, but such groups in Canada do not enjoy either the local and financial backing or the access to the media that they have in the United States.

Nonetheless, the founding of the Reform Party and its great success in the 1993 and 1997 federal elections causes concern at many levels of Canadian politics. Although Reform's rhetoric and platform are right-wing populist and western nationalist, its inner circle of decisionmakers are urban and professional with aspirations to woo and serve big capital. In 1992, the party campaigned for the "no" vote in the federal referendum on the Charlottetown Accord to amend the constitution to satisfy Quebec. In the 1997 election, it campaigned forcefully on a "tough love" platform of opposition to any recognition of distinct-society status for Quebec. Reform's stance appealed to resentment toward the Roman Catholicism, "special pleading," and the "foreignness" of Quebec.

At the same time, Manning and his followers have attacked parliamentary institutions, including the Senate, for being unelected, ineffective, and unequal. This is an issue of broad appeal, reflecting traditional criticism from democrats and populists of all parties in Canada. Reform's members of Parliament have renounced as unnecessarily privileged the lavish retirement provisions accorded all members. Although the party is rigidly controlled by Manning himself, it has advocated placing some policy questions directly before grassroots constituency meetings. At the same time, it advocates entrenching property rights in the constitution's Charter of Rights and Freedoms, and its platform explicitly endorses free enterprise. Under the guise of libertarian reasoning and strict interpretation of deficit control, Reform has emerged as a bastion of the (white, middle class, nuclear) family, tax reduction, immigration restrictions, increased military spending, and opposition to public funding of the arts and of public broadcasting, to gun control, and to most social spending.

As the 1993 election wiped out the Progressive Conservative Party in Parliament, Reform reaped the benefit of western voter hostility. The party's elected members jumped from one to fifty-four, more than the NDP ever held. In view of Canadian history it is unlikely that Reform will be able to win support from big capital, prevent the reconstruction of the Conservatives, and gain electoral support outside the West. But in the 1997 election, its sixty-seat support was solid enough to make Reform the official opposition, which in the parliamentary system has a veto function comparable to that of the U.S. presidency in its relation to Congress.

Many see this crystallization of right-wing hostility to changing social conditions and threats to established assumptions as a portent of the assault on liberal democracy and equality already evident in Europe and the United States—possibly even as a return of fascism. Manning and his followers are far better organized and politically sophisticated than the traditional, spontaneous populist movements from the west such as the Progressive Party, Social Credit, and the cooperative movement. Reform's aspiration is to replace the Progressive Conservative Party and become an explicitly right capitalist alternative to the Liberals. This goal is similar to that of the group—from Barry Goldwater to Ronald Reagan—which transformed the U.S. Republican Party from moderate conservatism to the rallying point for the far right.

Issue Organization

The existence of ideological and subordinate class parties in Canada traditionally diminished the importance of pressure group politics. Such parties express some of the characteristics of grassroots movements, offering an alternative to what are often referred to as the "brokerage" parties.

In the context of parliamentary policymaking, party discipline is much stronger than in the U.S. political system. As a result, individual members of Parliament have less power than a U.S. senator or congressperson can amass. Powerless backbench MPs have traditionally been unattractive to business pressure groups. Moreover, MPs in the cabinet must win support for policy initiatives from a majority of their colleagues. Parliamentary committees, always controlled by the government, have less power than their congressional counterparts and are not usually policy-initiating bodies. As executive rather than legislative power has increased, public relations specialists and lobbyists (frequently subsidiaries of U.S. firms) have proliferated in Ottawa and the provincial capitals, concentrating their efforts on the bureaucracy as well as elected ministers. As in the United States (indeed in all liberal democracies) it is the business community that enjoys the greatest access to such professional talent and therefore the greatest influence on policy.

Since the Second World War the Canadian state, federally and provincially, has funded voluntary organizations. No equivalent practice exists in the United States, though tax exemptions, mailing privileges, and other subsidies have long been available to politically approved causes. Millions of budgetary dollars are distributed each year in Canada to every conceivable kind of organization devoted to socially desirable projects, so long as they are not engaged in partisan political advocacy.

One governmental purpose of this distribution is to assure co-optation and surveillance, but it has also sustained specific-interest organizations, many of which have been aggressive advocates of popular causes. In the recent years of austerity such organizations have discovered that they can no longer rely on state funding, which implies greater autonomy but also a tenuous existence—as illustrated by the February 1995 federal budget, which cut back funding for the semigovernmental Canadian International Development Agency. When the agency decided to devote its remaining assets exclusively to foreign aid projects, the result was that a vast array of voluntary community organizations involved in education and support for third world development across Canada were summarily abolished.

Although trade unions, funded by members, have always been politically vocal, they have channeled their social and legal demands through political parties. Peace organizations throughout the century have also sought to influence political parties and to work through factions within parties. More recently, women's organizations and environmental groups have effectively pursued their objectives independent of political parties and governments, continually targeting all those in power as well as public consciousness.

In the late 1960s, a left-wing economic nationalist movement, the Waffle, emerged within the New Democratic Party. (Legend has it that the name was coined when one of the founders joked that it would be best to "waffle to the left" rather than to the right.) Originating among young people who were anti-imperialist and hostile to the Vietnam War, it resembled the U.S. new left. In contrast, however, its goals were economic independence from U.S. domination and a socialist Canada. It found fertile ground among many NDP members and among rank-and-file trade unionists, even receiving formal backing of some locals, despite vigorous opposition from most union leaders. Yet after a short career it was isolated and expelled from the party, then vanished as a movement.

Change of Political Players and Attitudes

Since the struggle in the early 1980s to patriate the British North America Act as the Canadian constitution, there has been significant change in the party-parliamentary character of politics. Two attempts to amend the constitution to satisfy Quebec foundered, primarily for lack of democratic procedure. In 1982, a strong, independent women's formation, the National Action Committee on the Status of Women (NAC), which had developed throughout the 1970s, revolted against the exclusion of popular groups from the negotiations over reform of the constitution. The process was restricted to the provincial premiers and the prime minister, including their principal—mostly male—civil servants. No provision was made for popular consultation or ratification. The NAC mounted a powerful lobbying effort and forced women's rights to be embedded in the new Charter of Rights and Freedoms, a critical component of the new constitution.

Indigenous peoples have taken the same route as women in organizing powerful, autonomous national representation; so have disabled and elderly people. The most recent attempt to amend the constitution, the Charlotte-town Accord in 1992, did include greater public consultation but was still rejected in a referendum, primarily because of popular criticism of the restrictive procedures deriving from the conservative, paternalistic, parliamentary political culture Canada has inherited.

The change occurring in the social and political process is not easy to define. In most countries executive government has become stronger. Throughout the liberal democratic world, political parties and politicians are under attack because of the absence of democracy in the decision-making process. Traditional assumptions of liberalism are under attack as no longer relevant and unnecessarily burdensome. In Canada, this has not yet resulted, as in the United States, in a retreat from the civic process or a sharp polarization between affluent participants and poor abstainers. But new and nontraditional means of popular power are sought, with specific issue groups targeting both corporate and governmental power. But perhaps because of the feeling that they can participate in civil life with some meaningful effect, opinion sampling continues to indicate that in comparison with other capitalist countries, Canadians are relatively content with their political system. In March 1994, for example, an international survey by the Times Mirror Company found that 44 percent of Canadians believed that their governing body had "a good influence on the way things are going." That figure was only 23 percent for Germany, 27 percent for Britain, and 39 percent for the United States. Nevertheless, as early as the struggle over patriation of the constitution in 1982, politicians perceived a popular loss of respect for politics. This impression intensified after the 1992 constitutional referendum defeat, and then the 1993 election in which the Tories were reduced to two seats in the House of Commons. Politicians may be right to worry, for the same Times Mirror survey reported that 35 percent of Canadians felt that Parliament had "a mainly bad influence on the way things are going." (The remaining 21 percent indicated neither, both, or no opinion.) Americans were more decisively alienated: 44 percent regarded Congress as a bad influence.[2]

Although by no means complete or conclusive, such evidence speaks to the issue of legitimacy so crucial to the liberal democratic system of class rule. With the removal of the "Iron Curtain" symbol of anti-democracy, lack of freedom, and the tyrannical and arbitrary rule ascribed to Communist countries, capitalist politicians can no longer rely on public affirmation of electoral democracy as the best and only alternative. Increasingly, people seem restless with conventional governmental channels. During the 1980s and 1990s, Canadian politicians faced spontaneous and independent issue organizations that they could not easily co-opt, as they had done in a more compliant past.

The Canadian Labour Congress (CLC), for example, has given formal recognition to the development of more grassroots and participatory democracy by proclaiming its desire to develop coalitions with other popular formations. In August 1994 the Canadian Auto Workers proclaimed:

> The union model we are reaching for emphasizes not just militancy but deepening the role of the union in the workplace and in the lives of its membership. This model acknowledges the importance of "social unionism" but recognizes the need to move on to "movement unionism." It points toward coalition-building but it also suggests that the first steps toward understanding the diversity of workers across regions and sectors must include a measure of that diversity within our own structures. And to keep this altogether, we need to have a clearer ideology of what we're about—a philosophy and a vision that challenges the dominant perspectives in our society.[3]

This approach by organized labor, especially public-sector workers, to relate its campaigns to wider community and issue organizations has resulted in large and broad mobilizations. Following the Ontario NDP government's defeat by a right populist Conservative Party in 1995, the provincial budget and the NDP's pro-labor legislation, as well as social programs including health and education, were slashed. In response, the labor movement together with community and people's organizations mounted a series of day-long general strikes held consecutively in large cities throughout the province. All were massively attended, resulting in the virtual closing of each city during the strike. And in May and June 1996, the labor movement together with the NAC organized a trek from Vancouver to Ottawa, mobilizing hundreds of thousands to protest budgetary restraints and program cuts and to demand renewal of social services, particularly for the poor and women.

It might be thought that the primary beneficiary of the popular revolt against formal political parties would be the NDP, which has historically represented itself as the most democratic of Canada's political parties. Instead, however, the NDP at both federal and provincial levels, whether in government or in opposition, has exhibited the rigidities and resistance to internal democracy common to social democratic and Communist parties the world over. In the 1990s the NDP has been regarded with suspicion by people's movements and seen as an impediment to the reforms they seek. Even the labor movement, whose own bureaucratic and centralist history inspires little enthusiasm among democrats, today finds itself in conflict with the party that was supposed to be its political arm. The conflict emerged not only for reasons of social and economic policy but also because of the failure of NDP governments to extend or practice democracy in civil services and crown corporations (state-run industries) and because of the party's attempts to co-opt group causes and leadership in order to manage their agendas.

The fight against the U.S.-Canada Free Trade Agreement and the aftermath election of the NDP in Ontario provides a clear example of the changes in the means of political struggle. The emerging cooperation of people's organizations that began in the 1970s was given a boost in 1983 by the radical statement of the Canadian Conference of Catholic Bishops advocating greater attention to the plight of the poor and of workers. A laborious process of coalition-building continued through the 1980s until the free trade issue emerged clearly. In 1987, the Pro-Canada Network was formed to fight the issue and coordinate the resistance of some thirty-two national organizations, among them the CLC, the NAC, the National Farmers' Union, the left-nationalist Council of Canadians, and Gatt-Fly, a church-based peace and development organization. As Leo Panitch and Donald Swartz noted:

> It was the remarkable national political intervention of this coalition that largely turned the 1988 federal election into a referendum on free trade. In the process, it set the terms of the debate, defining "Canadianism" precisely in terms of support for those aspects of the welfare state so absent south of the border, and thus providing a strong ideological basis for defensive struggles, not only against free trade but also the broader parameters of what came to be known as the "corporate agenda."[4]

The leaders of many of these organizations were socialists, and not a few were among the cadre of the NDP elected in Ontario in 1990, many as first-time candidates.

Since the 1980s, the neoliberal state and the individualist egoism of libertarian ideology have increased their claim for hegemony. Historically, both the conservative organic view of society and the individual and socialist communal collectivism have exerted a decisive, if not hegemonic, influence in Canada. The major "brokerage" parties, which are based upon forming coalitions of disparate interests throughout the country, are substantially unaffected by neoliberalism. They have always eschewed ideology and adopted issues pragmatically, shifting to right or left as they interpreted the moods of funders and voters. The idea of a marketplace of interests—the more the merrier—is congenial to them.

Much less enthusiastic about the multiplication of specific-interest organizations in Canada and in Europe are the more explicitly class-based and ideologically prone parties, which have been hard hit in the present environment. In Canada, the NDP has seen its support eroded in favor of particular-interest organizations, which in turn have developed structures nationwide in scope and bent upon focused reforms but not yet sufficiently coherent among themselves to create a party of social change. Meanwhile, the triumphal assertions of neoliberalism and globalization have become so dominant that the media and their anointed pundits have lost sight of the stagnation of real economic life. What William Tabb says in reference to the United States applies to Canada as well:

> The current offensive of capitalist logic into all realms of social life undermines many of the legitimation functions of the state which have provided citizen loyalty for the accumulation patterns of the capitalist system. The demand that everything be done through the market . . . represent[s] [an attack] on programs which have broad support. But the self-confidence with which market ideologists attack any sense of public space, of solidaristic provision of services and shelter from the relentless individualistic values of the market, represents a measure of the defeat of democracy.[5]

Chapter 8

Stagnation and Neoliberalism

Capitalist economies in the era of monopoly are ever prone to stagnation; they do not grow and reproduce automatically. This was particularly clear to economists and governments, not to mention masses of working people, during the Great Depression. The Second World War stimulated renewed growth that seemed unending to some. After the 1960s, however, capitalist economies faltered, slowed, and today are stagnant with short spurts of growth and long periods of little or no growth. The rise of a politics of neoliberalism corresponds to these economic conditions.

The Second World War provided Canada, like the United States, with economic stimulation for recovery from depression, re-employment, infra-structure renewal, and mass consumption. Unlike the United States, Canada did not embark on an international diplomatic and military buildup, nor did it launch into European reconstruction spending. Canada's own financial community did export capital to traditional markets in the Caribbean, the United States, and Britain but not on the scale in which U.S. business launched itself into world markets.

In the twenty-five years of economic expansion following the war, Canada's two major political parties were driven by conflicting ideological tendencies and growth strategies. The primary forces within the Conservatives were oriented to Great Britain and viewed the United States balefully; their leader in the 1960s, John Diefenbaker, had already clashed with President Kennedy over the Cuba crisis. The Liberals were led by Lester Pearson, and the dominant influences within his party pursued a "continentalist" policy, seeing trade with the United States and cordial relations in international affairs as the most fruitful strategy for "a middle power." Yet another, more economic-nationalist wing of the Liberal Party was wary of the preponderant influence of American capital.

During the 1960s, the American war in Vietnam troubled a wide range of Canadians, who take the United Nations Charter much more seriously than Americans do. Prime Minister Pearson, who had won the Nobel Peace Prize in 1957, symbolized dominant public opinion on the appropriate role of Canada: promoting international peace. As the war dragged on, more and more American draft evaders and then deserters poured into Canada with the active assistance of ordinary citizens, churches, universities, and community groups. Despite adverse reaction from the U.S. government, the Canadian government refused to prohibit the flow; the RCMP monitored this social movement but did not disrupt it. At the same time, public identification of the United States as an imperialist power became more common. The growth of repugnance was remarkable, since Great Britain had been an empire and Canada part of it; the mere fact of imperialism was not particularly reprehensible to Canadians. (In contrast, prior to the start of the Cold War, imperialism—especially colonialism—had been anathema to a significant portion of the American public: many had opposed the acquisition of former Spanish colonies after 1900; Scott Nearing's book *Dollar Diplomacy* was a bestseller in the 1920s and 1930s.) By the 1960s, however, the oppressive and exploitative character of U.S. international behavior came widely under criticism and condemnation in Canada, as elsewhere.

Both the increasing concern over U.S. corporate ownership of the Canadian economy and aversion to the manifestations of U.S. imperialism gave rise to nationalism within the Anglo-Canadian population. At the same time, Quebec was experiencing the Quiet Revolution, which fostered its own brand of nationalism together with a province-building economic development strategy. This surge of nationalism in two different manifestations—Anglo and Quebec—extended from the 1960s into the 1970s. The federal Liberal government and the provincial NDP governments in Manitoba and Saskatchewan adopted mildly nationalist policies by creating crown corporations and investment regulation agencies and by adopting nationalist rhetoric in their political platforms. Prime Minister Trudeau briefly suggested that Canada should withdraw from NATO, and he even went so far as to praise the welfare state advocated by John Kenneth Galbraith.

After 1973, however, economic nationalism was shoved aside in favor of controlling inflation and stimulating the economy. Rising inflation was less acceptable than in previous decades, now that the economy and profits had ceased to grow. As the reality of "stagflation" became more apparent, the federal government's attempts to cope meant, in the first instance, wage and price controls that sharpened class conflict and struggle, and, in the second instance, government-induced mega-projects intended to stimulate investment. These included development of the vast heavy-oil and oil sands deposits in western Canada; the opening of oil exploration in the high Arctic, the Beaufort Sea, and the Hibernia field off the east coast of Newfoundland; and the launching of giant hydroelectric projects in Quebec, Ontario, Manitoba, and British Columbia.

Corporate leadership, for its part, during the 1970s abandoned the agreement that had stabilized all advanced capitalist economies for thirty years. There had long been rhetoric in the business community lamenting big government, intrusive government, free-spending government, the coddling of welfare bums, and the like. Despite this voice, in the decades following the Second World War, business, labor, and government had reached an informal agreement that wages would rise without undue disruption of production; output volume and prices would increase to assure rising profits; and government would conduct a social service system to sustain the social reproduction of labor, prop up the income system, and mediate a balance of class benefits. Broadly, this was a corporatist solution reached, with different particulars, in all the advanced capitalist countries—except perhaps the United States, which relied heavily on military spending to achieve stimulus and distribution.

But as profit margins narrowed under the effects of rising energy costs, inflation, and diminishing opportunities for profitable investment in manufacturing and resources, capital sought massive reductions in the costs of production, government spending, and taxes. Gradually the archaic "theories" of the "free market," laissez-faire, entrepreneurship, the rational and calculating consumer, and particularly the idea that the cost of big social spending by government is unwarranted all came back into fashion and then became dogma.

This ideology proceeded earliest and fastest in British and American professional economics. Establishment research institutes in Canada in the 1970s included the private C. D. Howe Institute and the Economic Council of Canada, a government-funded body until 1992.[1] Both of these high-profile think tanks were slow to adopt the neoliberal strategies, but the right-wing Fraser Institute in Vancouver, an ideological subsidiary of the overdeveloped genre in the United States, bombarded the Canadian intellectual and policy community with nostrums. These included the miracles to be achieved by privatization of crown corporations, elimination of government budget deficits by downsizing, the freeing of the individual to pursue rational self-interest, the evils of the graduated income tax, and the benefits to flow from unrestrained capital investment and profit seeking.

Behind the stream of neoliberal conventional wisdom that gradually penetrated Canada in the 1980s, replacing the conventional wisdom of the Keynesian compact, two important developments were reshaping capitalism. The first was the emergence of financial capital as a source of profit greater than industrial and raw-material production. The second was the global restructuring of capitalist organization, which embraced all advanced industrial countries. Beginning in the mid-1970s and proceeding at an increasing pace, international commerce in financial instruments ballooned into the tens of trillions and then hundreds of trillions of dollars per year. At the same time, commerce in industrially produced and natural-resource commodities remained relatively stable at between $2 and $3 trillion per year. Making money from the circulation of money was facilitated by the explosion in electronic technology, as well as by narrowing control over financial and industrial resources to multinational banks and corporations. Obviously, release from controls and regulations by governmental agencies and rules was a high priority for institutions of private capital that could now make the entire globe (temporarily excluding the Communist bloc) their marketplace.

During the final term of the Trudeau Liberals in the early 1980s, government policy began to focus on heightened concern about budgetary deficits, the Bank of Canada's monetary conservatism, transfer of fiscal responsibility for social programs to the provinces, and unilateral curtailment of equalization payments to those provinces. As a result of these measures, and of conflicts between federal and provincial governments (none of which were Liberal) surrounding the patriation of the constitution, hostility to the Trudeau Liberals became severe. In 1984, business shifted its support from the Liberals to the Tories in an unprecedented flood of 80 percent. Liberal defeat that year ushered in a national sigh of relief and the start of adoption of the Thatcher-Reagan neoliberal strategy.

Despite Brian Mulroney's election promises to heal the angers produced by Trudeau, his government soon attacked old-age pensions, producing a large and vocal response from the community of senior citizens and a humiliating retreat by the new government. So extensive in scope and depth had the Canadian social security system become and so precious to the electorate that its degradation seemed virtually unthinkable. (By contrast, in the United States the 1995 Republican Congress made a sweeping attack on welfare, designed to save $65 billion and destroy the system, part of its "Contract with America.")

Meanwhile, for the first time in Canadian history, a pressure group of the largest domestic and international banks and corporations was formed: the Business Council on National Issues.[2] Unlike the Canadian Manufacturers' Association and the Chamber of Commerce, both large but diverse agglomerations of capital which had been in existence for many years, BCNI concentrated interests and organization in a relatively small but rich and powerful group of Canadian and American capitalists concerned with international trade. It was modeled on the Business Roundtable in the United States, but made up in large part of representatives of the biggest U.S. firms operating in Canada. Its objectives were twofold: to change the dominant discourse of Canadian public life, and to hitch Canada to the global restructuring process.

Prime Minister Mulroney, who had entered office declaring his opposition to a free-trade agreement with the United States, was soon converted to principal spokesman for such a strategy. Each subsequent yearly budget, moreover, proclaimed the solemn duty of the government to reduce the relentless rise in budget deficits. All other social priorities had to bow before the need to confront this looming catastrophe. Soon no public institution in Canada could justify itself without genuflecting before the altar of budget reduction: schools and universities; the health system; public works and construction; public transportation; municipal, provincial, and federal government departments without exception; museums, art galleries, and symphony orchestras. Every aspect of life was affected—except, of course, grants, subsidies, rebates, and loan guarantees to private business, the supposed engine of prosperity. (During the same era Americans were experiencing an even more grotesque inflation of spending on the military, bailouts for savings and loan companies, and tax giveaways to the rich.)

Yet the Canadian federal budget deficits began to rise in 1980, from $12.7 billion in 1981 under a Liberal government to $45 billion by the end of the Tory government in 1993. Using standard methods of capitalist debt financing, the accumulating debt ate up more and more of state revenues in interest service. The deficit and debt also contributed to double-digit inflation in interest rates to attract domestic and foreign speculators. Further, they tended to depress the value of the Canadian currency in the international money market, thereby attracting adverse judgments from Wall Street bond-rating agencies and the International Monetary Fund, whose criticisms further increased the cost of borrowing. In 1990, the IMF pressured the Conservative government to freeze the wages and salaries of federal government employees; that freeze remained in effect during the subsequent Liberal regime. The international agency also expressed its discontent with the $25 billion budget cut in 1995, urging ". . . additional savings from the further reform of Canada's unemployment insurance system and other social programs." Canada's representative on the IMF, Douglas See, was reported as saying that "the federal fiscal strategy for eliminating the deficit is fully in line with the IMF's recommendations."[3]

It became increasingly clear that neoliberal policies adopted in the United States and the United Kingdom were to be installed in Canada. The most important institutional goal of the BCNI was a free trade agreement with the United States, which they hoped would curtail for the foreseeable future the ability of Canadian governments to restrict the movement of capital, forestall government regulation of economic activity, and reverse the expansion or even maintenance of social programs. In the two years leading up to the 1988 election, the free trade agreement gradually became the exclusive issue on which the campaign would be fought. In the process the BCNI and the federal Progressive Conservative Party became indistinguishable.

In the middle of the nineteenth century a reciprocal trade agreement with the United States had been signed but later abrogated. In 1911, the Liberal government of Sir Wilfred Laurier went down to defeat for espousing a tariff reduction agreement with the United States on less than a quarter of cross-border trade. His government was sunk by the opposition's slogan, "No truck or trade with the Yankees." But by the 1980s, nationalism within the capitalist class had, for all intents and purposes, vanished. The rationale for a free trade agreement was that the United States was becoming more protectionist under intensifying competition from Japan and Europe and that Canada had a momentary opportunity to strike a deal that would guarantee exemption from the protectionist policies the United States was bound to initiate. In a restructuring global economy, Canada would have to act quickly to assure preferred access to its principal market.

Following the lead of BCNI strategists, then, all Canadian federal and provincial governments successfully enshrined deficit-cutting as paramount policy. This made it necessary to alter the content of the dominant ideology from meeting social needs and healing domestic divisions to becoming internationally competitive by eliminating the deficit. During the same period, a regime of stern monetarism established by the Bank of Canada retained double-digit interest rates even though inflation was declining to 1 percent or less. Only in 1995, after more than a year of negligible inflation, did interest rates drop to 3 percent. High interest rates discouraged both consumer and business borrowing and therefore spending and job creation. Consequently, despite recurrent government promises, during the 1980s deficit reductions could never be achieved because of high unemployment and the high cost of borrowing. Indeed, whatever the political rhetoric, no government in the 1980s could achieve balanced budgets. In Canada, as in Europe, that failure points up the danger to ruling class legitimacy posed by draconian attacks on social programs. Deficit reduction and elimination in the past decade has been achieved only by abandoning responsibility for programs, cutting entitlements and services, and eliminating programs altogether—in short, by denigration of the standard of living.

Given the Canadian social safety net developed over forty years, a depressed economy multiplied the social expenses of public welfare. The stagnant economy in the 1980s therefore generated opposition to government policy. Unlike the United States, Canada does not have high military costs perpetually built into its budgets, or the costs associated with managing an empire. But the budgetary costs of equalizing social programs were structural and had previously been beyond the unilateral control of the federal government. Thus, actions by the federal government to thrust social-program costs back onto provincial budgets without commensurate relaxation of centralized taxing led to heightened conflicts in federal-provincial relations. Attempts starting in the early 1980s to dilute and dismember parts of the universal health, education, and welfare system originally met with less success than expected, and throughout the Conservatives' second term in power, 1988 to 1993, their popular support plummeted. Conservative governments were defeated in all but two provinces. This meant continuing resistance from provincial governments when the federal government sought to offload budgetary responsibilities or change the terms and conditions of negotiated programs.

The Conservative government was prevented from destroying the network of social programs built over forty-five years, but not by the opposition Liberal and NDP parties in Ottawa—in fact, despite a change to a Liberal government in 1993, the cuts not only continued but became more extensive. Rather, the Conservatives were stymied by popular mobilization of specific-issue groups in the 1980s. As already noted, trade unions, particularly in the public sector, lobbied and bargained federally and provincially in support of social legislation. The National Action Committee on the Status of Women was aggressive and effective in its agitation for programs to support women, children, and families. The elderly and disabled were organized as never before to protect programs of particular importance to them. Indigenous Canadians organized during the 1980s, extensively and effectively, to secure control over land owed to them; to take control away from the paternalistic and oppressive federal administration of fishing, hunting, health, welfare, and education; and to secure legal recognition of their right to self-government. Environmental groups, especially Greenpeace, were effective in high-profile campaigns to force even the Tory government to improve standards and enforcement in the boundary waters and transborder air pollution, despite resistance from the Reagan administration.

The balance of class forces in Canada distinguished its economic, political, and social-policy debates and actions from the United States. For one thing, the achievement of "entitlements" had been more extensive and inclusive and the mobilization of popular and political defense of them was more widespread—pan-Canadian. This reflects the relative weakness of the Canadian ruling class in comparison with that of the United States, not simply ideologically but in its command of the state and in its ability to transfer the costs of economic restructuring onto the subordinate classes. It also reflects the significance of a culture of values more communal than individualist. Yet the relentless, blind pressure of global (but especially American) financial interests eventually forced compliance from Canadian economic and political leaders.

During 1996 and 1997, Canada's economy improved at the same time that the federal government reduced its budget for public spending. In anticipation of an election, the predicted budget deficit declined from 25 percent in 1996 to 19 percent in 1997. As the election drew nearer, the year-end deficit sank to a predicted 9 percent. Some economists asserted that it had already vanished and that by the end of the year the austerity plan would produce a budget surplus, which several provinces had already achieved. Just as inflation was "cured" not by neoliberal economic strategies but by unemployment, so the budget deficit bogey was licked by budgetary stringency on social programs.

However satisfactory the neoliberal ideological project has been for capitalists and their ruling parties, it has failed to restore social and national prosperity in Canada. In 1997, unemployment remained stubbornly high at just below 10 percent, a fact acknowledged by the governor of the Bank of Canada, at the same time, ironically, that he warned of increased interest rates. Free trade has not brought the foreign investment that its advocates predicted, nor has it provided easy Canadian access to the U.S. market. Its important achievement in Canada has been to convince governments to diminish socially beneficial welfare, health, education, culture, and environmental protection programs by transferring authority, without sufficient funding, for these programs to the provinces. Provincial governments of all political coloration have learned the lesson and dumped service responsibilities onto municipal governments. At the same time, corporate executive remuneration has become obscenely generous without commensurate change in tax schedules to transfer such wealth to the public purse. In short, stagnation and its neoliberal rationale have succeeded in reducing the standard of living of the many for the benefit of the privileged few.

Chapter 9

The Crisis of Canadian
Social Democracy

Since the nineteenth century, political economy has explained and contested the inadequacies and failures of capitalist strategy and policy, mostly from the socialist perspective. But in the present period socialist theory has been thrust to the margins, and socialist political practice has widely abandoned its roots.

On the U.S. left, many have looked upon Canada's New Democratic Party with admiration as a model for an equivalent formation in the United States. When in office, the NDP was responsible for creating and extending social programs and assisting labor; as the opposition party it carried the demands of subordinate classes—all this without a doctrinaire political ideology. During the postwar period of economic growth, social legislation and improved living standards for the middle and lower classes were advocated and achieved without substantial interference in the system of capitalist development. Since the 1970s, however, social democracy has been in decline, and in the 1993 federal election the NDP faced extinction. The decline of social democracy does not mean the imminent demise of such parties in the capitalist centers, but rather the end of the reformist strategies that originally defined them.

Since the Co-operative Commonwealth Federation's inception as a national political movement and party in the 1930s and then in provincial government in the 1940s, the strategies of Canadian social democracy have been the building of local infrastructure (rural electrification, hospitals and schools, roads, transportation and communication systems), the mobilization of subcentral revenue, financial integrity, and the provision of social programs for the entire community, especially those least able to purchase their own services. As the party of provincial government or in opposition from 1944 until the 1980s, the CCF/NDP was responsible for building the infrastructure of provinces, nationalizing such services as auto and health insurance, adopting pro-labor industrial relations legislation, nationalizing selected natural resource extraction, and adopting environmentally protective policies.

Social democracy in Canada accepts the North American interpretation of electoral democracy: one person, one vote. Each individual is approached as an isolate, wooed to donate a single vote once every five years to the NDP. The CCF's original collectivist idea of a party as the instrument of a cluster of communities with certain common purposes is now anathema in the NDP. By the 1990s, NDP platforms had become dubious collections of bonbons for the numberless plurality of supposed tastes among the fickle electorate.

In the present crisis, moreover, the federal party and the provincial parties have been freed from responsibility to traditional constituencies in the subordinate classes. This is now most evident in Ontario, where private-sector trade unions, though not entirely satisfied with the NDP government between 1990 and 1995, nevertheless got enough of what they wanted to continue supporting the party; public-sector service unions, on the other hand, renounced their tie to the NDP because of its complicity in slashing the wages and jobs of public employees. For many in the popular movements who retain a socialist agenda, the NDP has become more a problem than a solution, an impediment to getting on with the creation of a socialist formation. But for many in the west facing a surge of right-wing Reform support, it is seen as the only alternative. Similarly, in the Maritimes, exasperation with Liberals and Tories resulted in election of eight provincial NDP candidates in 1997, and in March 1998, the NDP tied the governing Liberals in Nova Scotia for provincial seats, a startling event in a province that, in its 130 years' existence, had elected only Liberals and Tories.

Beginning with Saskatchewan Farmers

When social democracy was launched nationally in the 1930s, capitalism was in systemic crisis on a scale never before experienced. The CCF at both the federal and provincial levels demanded fundamental change in Canadian society. Its program called for a planned, socialized economy: socialization of banking, currency, credit and insurance, transportation, communications, and electric power; security of tenure for farmers; a national labor code, a universal pension system, and unemployment insurance; socialized health services; and other steps that would alter social organization. Organizationally, the federal party was a collection of local and provincial constituency organizations, clubs, and grassroots groups, including some from labor, the co-ops, and teachers. All its funds were voluntarily donated by its members and allies. Campaigns were conducted by volunteers, and paid workers were few.

The party's first electoral success in 1944 occurred in Depression-wracked Saskatchewan, giving hope to socialists and apoplexy to capital. But disappointing electoral results in the 1930s had already caused party leaders to dampen socialist rhetoric and aspirations. Saskatchewan, one of the poorest and most devastated jurisdictions in North America as a result of the Depression, needed the kind of infrastructure-building and economic stimulation that a CCF government was prepared to supply. Its economy was based on wheat, much in demand during the war, but the financial and transportation systems were in the hands of big capital based in Toronto and Montreal. The Saskatchewan CCF represented family farmers (organized in cooperatives), schoolteachers, and a small urban, but scarcely unionized labor force. The religious community was divided roughly between Protestant supporters and Roman Catholic opponents of the CCF.

Not surprisingly, the CCF set its sights on constructing a physical infrastructure and a social support system to benefit poor farmers. Once in government, it provided one of the most extensive road systems in North America to assist a rural population of less than a million, dispersed over a cultivated area approximately the size of North and South Dakota, in getting its crop to market. The bankrupt private electric power and gas system was centralized into a government "crown corporation" which thereby assumed the bankruptcy and debt-servicing burdens of many small communities. Soon electric power was extended from cities to farms. The telephone system too was assembled into a crown corporation; small local private firms were bought out and replaced with a modern, technologically advancing service. A provincial bus and airline service was created to serve remote communities ignored by Greyhound and Trailways bus lines and by continental air routes. The first Canadian collective bargaining and progressive trade union legislation was based upon the U.S. Wagner Act. A professional civil service with collective bargaining rights was created. The first North American Arts Board was established to foster and fund professional and amateur arts. Further measures were designed to bring security and democracy to the educational system, to provide publicly funded hospital care, and to introduce a modern social welfare system. These indicate the scope of reform initiated in the first four-year term of the Canadian social democratic experiment.

In these reforms the government was fiscally prudent and, thanks to the general economic expansion, soon able to operate with budget surpluses. It set up a planning structure to coordinate administrative programs, though in the absence of an attack on the ownership of property, either in land or in capital, it could not be comprehensive social planning: the banks, the major international oil companies, the coal companies, transcontinental transportation, and the machinery companies—as well as family farmers—remained immune from socialization. Acceptable regulatory legislation was enacted, however, to provide some protection to Saskatchewan consumers and workers. All these steps were sufficient to ensure continued reelection of CCF governments from 1944 to 1964.

The final act of the Saskatchewan CCF, in 1962, was to introduce a comprehensive single-payer medical insurance system financed through consolidated tax revenues. The resulting political reaction was fierce. Adamant opposition came from the medical profession, with aggressive assistance from the American Medical Association. A small group—largely urban, middle class advocates of private medicine, led by the Liberal leader of the opposition— even threatened insurrection against the CCF government with a march on the legislature. Opposition leader Ross Thatcher, in a staged photo-op, pretended to kick in the legislature doors. It was one of the sharpest conflicts over a class question the province had witnessed.

In fact, the health system introduced in Saskatchewan and later adopted by the federal government for Canada as whole is not as thorough as that introduced by the Labour Party in Britain after the Second World War. It retains the sacrosanct proprietary provision of fee-for-service payment to private physicians, and the medical profession continues to control health provision and to supervise itself through professional colleges. But fee schedules are negotiated with provincial departments of health, and expansion or contraction of medical services and facilities is determined primarily by state policy. Preventive health services were not built into the system, and democratic user control over health services was explicitly rejected when the Saskatchewan CCF refused to sanction spontaneously created community health clinics. Soon doctors' opposition subsided, especially as they discovered that a state agency would guarantee more reliable payment than could be expected from private patients. Seeing the popularity of the CCF/NDP plan, in 1966 the federal Liberals brought in a national health insurance system, which was soon supplemented by similar programs in all provinces. Today all these programs are coordinated and reconciled through interprovincial ministerial policy negotiations, and common standards are enforced through the federal system of transfer payments.

Liberals in a Hurry

In the 1960s the social democratic program for transformation of Canada retreated from view. Until 1969, the party was able to govern only in Saskatchewan. In most provinces, organized labor's leadership gave the NDP its blessings but could not or would not deliver large-scale rank-and-file membership votes in heavily industrial provinces. Ideologically, the social democrats in the labor movement fought strenuously against a sectarian and deteriorating Communist Party, taking a Cold War anticommunist line scarcely distinguishable from that of the dominant Liberal Party. The federal CCF supported Canadian participation in the Korean War; NDP opposition to the Vietnam War was fragmentary and insubstantial. Individual members of Parliament extended their support to Cuba, but the NDP was almost invisible in peace and solidarity movements. So deeply was its leadership enmeshed in Cold War assumptions that it never addressed the growing domination of the Canadian political economy by American capital. During the 1960s it was the liberal wing of the Liberal Party in government that sounded the alarm about increasing U.S. capital control of the Canadian economy, and thereby deprived the NDP leadership of a potential ideological and electoral weapon. The socialist Waffle group seized the issue and attempted to persuade the NDP leadership, but its members were expelled from the party for their efforts. At the time of the 1970 FLQ crisis in Quebec, the parliamentary NDP split over support for the War Measures Act, a minority opposing but the majority supporting the Trudeau Liberals.

These are not isolated examples of social democratic acceptance of the bourgeois agenda. The NDP's orientation became exclusively electoral, with a dependence on opinion polls, public relations leadership in policy development, and fear of offending "conventional wisdom." This has hobbled the NDP's ability to build electoral support for a social democratic project, and also resulted in the "shopping list" of issues and proposals that the Liberal Party could co-opt without offending its capitalist patrons. Already by the early 1950s Prime Minister Louis St. Laurent had defined the CCF as "Liberals in a hurry." Yet however condescending this remark, it contrasted sharply in the same period with the hysterical U.S. editorial identification of social democracy with Communism.

In response to the weakening of a social democratic project for transformation in the federal NDP, a Canadian equivalent of the New Left of the 1960s emerged: the movement called, in mock self-derision, the Waffle. It was socialist and nationalist in its 1969 program, "For an Independent Socialist Canada." Most of the original signatories were young members of the NDP. Some had already achieved prominence, such as the University of Toronto economist Mel Watkins, who conducted the Liberal government analysis of the scope and significance of U.S. ownership of the Canadian economy. Their program called for extensive nationalization of capital, democratic reforms to political institutions, autonomy for Quebec, Canada's withdrawal from NATO, and a foreign policy independent of U.S. imperialism. The movement caught fire to such an extent that it panicked the leadership of the NDP. In 1971, the Waffle ran James Laxer, a young history professor, for party leader. He came in second to longtime CCF/NDP labor lawyer and party bureaucrat David Lewis, with more than a third of the convention vote. Shortly afterward, party officials and union bureaucrats, hoping to attract support from small business, successfully maneuvered to expel the Waffle organization from the NDP, and all its avowed members in Ontario with it.

Social Democratic Development

In 1969, the NDP was elected for the first time in Manitoba and two years later was returned to power in Saskatchewan. In both provinces new capital accumulation initiatives were introduced in a "province-building" strategy. In Saskatchewan, the potash industry was initially developed in the 1960s by private, mainly American, capital. When those companies rebelled against increased taxes, the new NDP government under Allan Blakeney set out to nationalize half the industry. Blakeney also created Saskoil, a provincial oil exploration and development company. (In these extensions of the state into capitalist markets the government was significantly influenced by pressure from the Waffle and other leftists within the party.) With the revenues from these resource companies, a crown investment company was inaugurated to seek joint-venture funding with private capital for uranium-mining options in northern Saskatchewan and, subsequently, oil and mineral investments in the Northwest Territories, Alberta, and British Columbia. A similar province-building strategy was adopted by the NDP government of Ed Shreyer in Manitoba, based upon large hydroelectric projects in the North (for power export to the United States) and a publicly-owned forest industry. Consistent with the familiar social democratic emphasis on service to the subordinate classes, both of these NDP governments expanded health, housing, and social service spending.

During the decade of the 1970s, the federal NDP, having rid itself of the Waffle, sought to renew its popular image by espousing a measure of economic nationalism. In the 1972 election campaign it attacked the wealth and privilege of big business under the slogan "corporate welfare bums," insisting that capital be forced to pay its fair share of taxes. Even so modest a platform won sufficient support to force an unofficial coalition government with the Liberals. Under pressure from the NDP, the federal Liberal government bought out some lesser private oil companies to form Petro-Canada and created a crown investment agency, the Canadian Development Corporation. In 1980, in response to forces within their own party, the Liberals set up the Foreign Investment Review Agency to screen new foreign investment in Canada. The NDP did not reap an electoral reward for its collaboration with the Liberals. Instead, in the 1974 election its seats fell from a historic high of thirty-one to sixteen.[1]

With the conclusion of the Vietnam War (an imperial defeat for the United States), the end of the UN Monetary and Financial Conference at Bretton Woods, and the combined development of high inflation and stagnant invest-ment, the social democratic alliance (as it has been dubbed by Samir Amin) began to unravel. The Keynesian fiscal and monetary techniques of state intervention in expanding capitalist economies to provide stimulation and restraint ceased to be effective during the 1970s. Lip service to full employ-ment policy was abandoned, and unemployment rose. The long-established tradeoff between rising wages and rising prices was abrogated. At the federal level the task of inflation control fell to Pierre Trudeau's Liberals, who introduced wage and price controls in 1975. In Saskatchewan, Allan Blakeney's NDP government willingly extended the same measures to provincial public-sector wages. Throughout his tenure as provincial party leader, Blakeney aggressively espoused the need to curtail the power of organized labor. It was primarily his effort to discipline labor as "just another pressure group" that brought about the NDP's 1982 election defeat in what should have been a certain victory.

Retrenchment

The 1980s are already notorious as the era of capital's counterrevolution against three and a half decades of social democratic reforms. The 1980s are also infamous for the failure of social democracy everywhere to revitalize itself with economic and social programs worthy to lead popular struggles. For Canada, the most pathetic example of this failure was the election of 1988.

If ever the NDP had a natural issue to seize and mobilize support around, it was opposition to free trade in the 1988 election. In the spring of that year, the NDP led the polls in popularity and its prospects to win the federal election or at least to form the official opposition seemed unbeatable. Public opinion showed that Mulroney and his Conservatives were falling steadily in popularity and the Canada-U.S. Free Trade deal was still more unpopular. NDP leader Ed Broadbent topped the polls as the most popular and trusted political leader. Organized labor strenuously opposed a free trade agreement, recognizing the adverse effect it would have on Canadian jobs. Much of the farm community opposed it as well, as did churches and virtually all women's, environmental, and other popular organizations. This was an issue that galvanized the intrinsic nationalist sentiment of Canadian ideology.

But the Progressive Conservative campaign strategy was to minimize the volatile issue because of its nationalistic content, and Broadbent initially accepted the definition of a campaign on domestic issues. In contrast, John Turner, leader of the Liberal opposition, grasped the free trade issue and made it the exclusive focus of the Liberal campaign. By summer NDP fortunes had wilted before a resurgence of the formerly despised Liberals. In October the PCs won with 43 percent of the vote while the opposition to free trade (always a majority of those polled) was split between Liberals (32 percent) and NDP (20 percent). Even in its own narrow terms of parliamentary electoralism, the NDP had failed miserably when offered a real chance to win federally—a message delivered to party leaders with vehemence by trade union spokesmen.

Still, the forty-three seats the NDP did win represented the largest number in their history, and the fight against free trade did not entirely evaporate. In October 1990, for the first time in Canada, an NDP government was elected in Ontario, the home of big capital. Within a year, however, that government was opposed not only by the two main parties that had ruled Ontario since its origin, but almost uniformly by the media, all business groups, and the civil service as well. It abandoned a promised public automobile insurance plan comparable to what is available in Saskatchewan, Manitoba, and British Columbia. Furthermore, NDP Premier Bob Rae's opposition to free trade, which had been high on the NDP's election platform, became no more than symbolic. The realities of budget deficits and accumulated debt, plus the unconcealed opposition of the entrenched senior civil service and an all-out rhetorical attack from business in general and the insurance industry in particular, persuaded the NDP leadership to retreat, despite its large popular mandate.

After the NDP brought down an expansionary budget in 1991, pressure from bond-rating houses in New York forced subsequent budget strategy to hew to the deficit-fighting orthodoxy of neoliberal monetarism. With the provincial economy in a slump that sent unemployment from 5 percent in 1989 to 11 percent in 1993, the NDP government introduced what it called Social Contract legislation—perhaps the most sweeping assault on trade union rights in Canadian history. Panitch and Swartz note:

> The government's unilateral framework for the Social Contract negotiations required, as a starting point, that the over 900,000 people employed in the broader public sector accept a three-year wage freeze, regardless of the terms of existing collective agreements. Moreover, in order to secure an actual reduction in the total wage bill of $2 billion during each of those years, it required an effective 5 per cent wage reduction through twelve days of 'unpaid leave' each year.[2]

Subsequently, despite overwhelming opposition in public negotiations, these were precisely the terms enacted in legislation. As Panitch and Swartz comment, "What has become particularly clear is that the NDP does not just fall short in terms of the degree of reform expected and needed by the unions, but that it can actively undermine union power and solidarity."[3]

After 1990, the NDP government in Ontario showed far more willingness to confront organized labor than either domestic or foreign capital. For a time after its election, the Rae government did express verbal opposition to the U.S.

and then the Mexican free trade agreement, especially because it is was responsible for the loss of some 400,000 jobs in the province. As Ontario's economic recovery improved in 1993, however, that verbal opposition faded. Thoroughly discredited, its members and supporters dispirited, the Rae government ran third in the 1995 provincial election, making way for a right-wing populist, neoliberal Conservative government.

Meanwhile, in the fall of 1991 NDP governments were elected in Saskatchewan and British Columbia which—with the already governing NDP in the North West Territories and Ontario—meant that a majority of Canadians were living under social democratic provincial governments. (Such a political fact in the aftermath of the "triumph of capitalism over communism" marks another difference from the United States.) British Columbia is usually one of the most prosperous resource-based provinces in Canada; Saskatchewan is usually among the poorest. When the NDP took office in British Columbia, its potential for state intervention in the economy was better than in most jurisdictions. It had not been necessary for the party to make campaign promises of any magnitude, since the electorate was strongly opposed to the long-ruling and corrupt Social Credit regime. Throwing out the rascals was enough in a province that was experiencing reasonable economic growth and an influx of Hong Kong investment. In Saskatchewan, too, popular revulsion against eight years of Progressive Conservative corruption was enough to get the NDP elected. But both the Ontario and British Columbia NDPs came to office with strong support from trade unions and popular movements for platforms promising traditional social democratic reforms. This was not the case in Saskatchewan.

Although virtually invisible to the U.S. public and marginal in Canadian affairs, Saskatchewan has a long social democratic history and is therefore significant as an example of the problems of social democracy in an era of neoliberalism. Social democratic parties throughout the world have resorted to removing obstreperous left formations by bureaucratic maneuvers and strong-arm tactics. But the Canadian CCF/NDP traditionally represented itself as different from major parties by virtue of its commitment to internal party democracy and leadership responsibility. As well, from the outset the movement contained a strong moral component, one foundation of the party's original attraction. Democracy was visible in the early CCF under the Saskatchewan and then federal party leadership of T. C. Douglas, a Baptist minister from the social gospel movement. However, his Saskatchewan successors, Allan Blakeney and Roy Romanow, abandoned the commitment to internal party democracy in favor of the autocratic style familiar in social democratic parties elsewhere (a style that, ironically, is not very different from that which they condemn in communist parties).

Thus, in this oldest and most reliable bastion of social democracy in North American history, the left was driven out of the party in the 1970s. First the center and then the right took virtually uncontested control during the 1970s and 1990s. Right-wing control became complete following a struggle that occurred during the first months of the newly elected government in 1991 over the party's stand on uranium mining. Northern Saskatchewan has the richest deposits of uranium in the world, and the NDP leadership has always wanted to sell it like any other mineral. But within the party there was strong grassroots, environmental, and antiwar opposition. A resolution adopted at an annual convention in the early 1980s had put the party on record as opposing nuclear development and uranium mining—a position similar to that taken by the British Columbia NDP. Within a month of his election in 1991 Premier Roy Romanow and his supporters decided to overturn the policy in order to attract investment. When the party convention defeated the attempt, the leadership mounted a major bureaucratic campaign within the membership which the following year was successful in abolishing the policy—and, predictably, alienating much of the remaining left, which opposed uranium mining.

A Neoliberal Future

The conflict over uranium also illustrated the shift of the Saskatchewan NDP toward appealing to the small-business community at the expense of an increasingly urban and working class constituency, with the exception of strong support from the United Steelworkers union organizing the uranium mines. Romanow is a lawyer, and his entourage is made up of lawyers, administrators, and other professionals. Their financial strategy, dominantly one of deficit fighting, has yielded such success that on a trip to Wall Street in June 1994 Romanow was welcomed enthusiastically by that financial community. The 1996 and 1997 budgets won accolades from the right-wing Fraser Institute think tank. The government's achievement is quite real. When Romanow entered office the provincial budget deficit was $842 million, which earned a bond rating of A3 in 1993. But the budget introduced in February 1995 projected a surplus of $119 million on a taxpaying population base of 400,000. By 1998, four successive budgets produced surpluses, importantly with the aid of lotteries, video lottery terminals, and casinos, which reverse the incidence of taxation from rich to poor. Such fiscal "good government" allowed the NDP to cut social programs enough to satisfy the bond market but not so severely as to prevent the party's reelection in 1996.

What appeared to impress investors was the NDP government's "reform" efforts to reorganize and downsize the health system. Demographic changes had made consolidation of health services long overdue, but the question of how it should be accomplished with minimal damage found the NDP adopting budgetary criteria on the side of administrators and against the interests of health workers and the general public. Moreover, in a province with an aging population there is increasing need for services and housing for senior citizens—and it must be remembered what a central role health and social services have played in the long history of Saskatchewan's social democracy. Yet instead of launching imaginative new programs to assist the aged, or even restoring old ones abandoned by the Conservatives, the government after 1991 set about forcing care back onto families and for-profit facilities. In addition, promised revision of labor legislation was watered down after protracted negotiations with the business community. Anti-scab provisions like those in Quebec since 1976 and those legislated by Ontario's NDP government were ignored in the face of business opposition. These examples indicate that the Saskatchewan NDP, the only North American social democratic party enjoying recurrent reelection, is extinguishing reform in favor of a neoliberal strategy congenial to Saskatchewan's business community and, of course, bond-rating agencies.

The Rise of Right Populism

After the electoral achievements at the provincial level in 1990 and 1991, it appeared to many that social democracy in Canada was about to break out of its historic third-party status. The label of "socialist" was no real impediment to the expectations of the NDP. The party was always anticommunist and had earned its Cold War credentials as a loyal, homegrown political formation against which redbaiting usually proved ineffective. When the Communist regimes of Eastern Europe collapsed, carrying with them the Communist parties in the West, the NDP was relieved of even the slight encumbrance of the socialist label.

In the year leading up to the federal election in 1993, popular opinion ran heavily against the governing Conservatives and especially against Prime Minister Brian Mulroney. Many thought this would be the time for the NDP to capitalize on its forty-three parliamentary seats. Instead, the Reform Party emerged as the voice of the petty bourgeois hinterland, denouncing big and irresponsible government controlled by "Eastern" forces, and demanding reduced government spending, support for the nuclear family, and the rest of the catalogue of familiar right-wing appeals. The strength of the Reform platform was a promise to make the Canadian governmental process democratic by continually consulting the people; this had been the populist social democratic appeal of the old CCF. Once again, the right-wing populist appeal caught the left-wing populists and social democrats unprepared. Reform's campaign was especially successful in British Columbia and Alberta; it also gained a few seats from Saskatchewan and Manitoba. The appeal helped destroy both the Progressive Conservative Party, which fell from 169 to 2 seats, and the NDP, which fell from 43 to 9. Under the rules of Parliament both parties were thereby deprived of official status, and the perquisites and media coverage entailed by that status. Business simply abandoned the Conservatives for the Liberals, as it had abandoned the Liberals in 1984, but the left and labor were denied any voice in government.

Since no popular movement now integrates the NDP with people's organizations, strategies, and priorities, this devastating electoral defeat signaled a major crisis for an organization with the putative aspiration of forming a federal government. For at least fifteen years the NDP has possessed no economic development strategy that the Liberal Party, with the support of a portion of big capital, cannot do better. Its electoral crisis of 1993 to 1997 meant that the NDP could not even perform its historic function as advocate and defender of the social safety net. The party has long been paralyzed by ambivalence about its relation with organized labor, fearing the identification, always seeking approval of "the ordinary man in the street" who, NDP leaders believe, resents the "special interests" (labor, indigenous peoples, the women's movement, ecologists, immigrants, gays, the elderly, the disabled) imagined to control the NDP. Equally paralyzing is the grip of electoralism, implying as it does the primacy of pollsters, spin doctors, and public relations, advertising, and media experts, all of whom cost more and more money.

In 1995 the now center-right Saskatchewan NDP easily won a second term in office, its opposition split between moribund and spiritless Liberals and Conservatives. In Ontario the Rae NDP, after alienating its working class constituency with neoliberal policies, ran third, defeated by the victorious Conservatives and opposition Liberals. In 1996 the British Columbia NDP, too, appeared headed for defeat when its leader was forced to resign over a corruption scandal. But his feisty successor, seeing no alternative, attacked his Liberal opponent on the grounds that he represented only the interests of the rich and privileged—the class issue. During its first term the NDP government had confronted the forest industry, long the most powerful economic force in British Columbia, and had taken significant steps to improve forestry practices, set aside virgin timber for wilderness areas, and include indigenous groups in resource management systems. In the election the NDP won a narrow victory, giving it a second term for the first time in British Columbia's history.

In the 1997 federal election, the NDP returned to full-party status in Parliament, winning 21 of the 301 seats. Its new leader, Alexa McDonough, conducted a spirited campaign on fundamental issues of jobs and protection of social programs that for the first time appealed especially to Atlantic Canada, where they won eight seats and received 38 percent of the regional vote. As usual, the NDP won no seats in Quebec; but it won no seats in Ontario (where many working class votes went Liberal or Reform), and only three seats in British Columbia (where most of its losses in mining and forest communities went to Reform).

The record of social democracy in Canada during the past fifty years has appealed to many on the U.S. left because of its accomplishments when in provincial office and because of its lack of dogmatic ideology and respect for democratic practice. Support for pro-labor legislation, advocacy of social programs beneficial to the subordinate classes with a minimum of humiliating bureaucratic regulation, legislative and judicial reforms to assist traditional victims of the state, the use of nationalized services and industries for the social rather than private good—all are part of the record to which the friends of social democracy on both sides of the border refer.

What has been overlooked is the drift toward paralysis. The wellsprings of vision, policy, and recruitment are dry. The social movement is deserting the NDP because the party has lost all functions save the contest of elections. Or, more accurately, the party has become fearful of the popular movement from which it arose, for people's organizations today will no longer permit the party to regulate their conduct as they search for new and relevant ideas, methods, and strategies.

Chapter 10

Searching for a Deeper Democracy

Canada in the 1990s appears to remain what it has long been: a rich dependency, a society like the United States in so many ways that it can be taken for granted by Americans and the world. Yet there are important differences for a citizenry that stubbornly resists amalgamation into the American melting pot.

The kinds of change that benefit capital inevitably dislodge those measures of protection and security, built under pressure from subordinate classes over long years of struggle, which ensure social cohesion. Thus, the changes engineered by big capital through the Conservative government of the 1980s and the Liberal government of the 1990s weakened the power of the Canadian state to play its traditional active, protective role; they also weakened the historic organizations and strategies of the popular agenda. Moreover, these changes in state, economy, and law, making Canada more vulnerable to international markets, are probably irreversible short of international economic collapse.

The economic development strategy of neoliberalism could not and did not produce growth and prosperity. It is reasonable to say that such a goal was not the purpose of the strategy. Instead, as in Britain and the United States, the monetarist, neoliberal strategy aimed at rolling back the entire structure of support, protection, regulation, stabilization, and compensation—the welfare state developed by Keynesian economists and social democratic politicians. The goal was to sweep away all the concessions wrung from capital in the postwar years of prosperity and to restore the predatory and vulnerable relationships that have always prevailed in the global periphery and for most of capitalist history in the metropolitan center.

Although such a complete counterrevolution was impossible in Canada between 1984 and 1997, major changes sought by international capital were achieved. First and most important, the two free trade agreements were imposed. Second, the ideological dominance of governmental deficit as a rationale for reducing the state's social responsibility was achieved. Third, the idea that as a trading nation Canada must convert itself entirely to the requirements of global competition has been established, though perhaps less securely. All three of these objectives now interrelate in such a way as to justify the capitalist agenda of reorganization of the Canadian economy and state. And they are accepted at least in principle by all the major parties.

In their 1993 electoral victory, the Liberals proclaimed their intention to renegotiate the free trade agreements and place priority on job creation. But these goals were soon replaced by efforts to extend free trade to Latin America, to restructure the social safety net, and, primarily, to reduce the budget deficit. As throughout the twentieth century, the capitalist class found no difficulty in switching its allegiance from the politically spent Conservatives back to a Liberal Party whose left wing has always been able to attract enough subordinate-class support to thwart the appeal of the NDP.

Adoption of the business agenda by all political parties has resulted in a resurgence of right-wing populism. The emergence of an organized right is neither unique nor unexplainable; it is common to all advanced capitalist societies (not to mention the former Communist system) that are restructuring under conditions of economic stagnation. As Daniel Singer wrote of Europe in 1994, "[W]e are probably moving towards a political confrontation, with the problem of employment, or rather unemployment, at the heart of the conflict. . . . It is an attempt by the employers to pass on the cost of the crisis to the workers."[1]

The relentless increase of capital accumulation, usually unaccompanied by real economic growth, occurs in all these countries without commensurate improvement for the general public in living standards or in the extension of democracy. Living standards for the masses in advanced capitalist countries are stagnant or declining. Where institutions, practices, and expectations of democracy are established, the discontent with capitalism's inequality among subordinate classes is channeled into avenues of reform deemed legitimate. The majority have reluctantly accepted capitalism's inequality in the hope of future improvement.

Greed and competition are the recognizable motive forces behind private accumulation. There is no such "automatic" motive force for the extension of democracy—broadly, the distribution and expansion of the power of the citizenry to effect governing decisions. The extension of democracy is the result of class struggles by organized social forces. In Canada, as in all liberal democratic societies, the forces accorded legitimacy to conduct that struggle are political parties. When they abandon the fight to extend democracy for society as a whole, other forces arise to restructure power relations according to their own interests. At the end of the twentieth century, the fight for democracy has been subordinated dramatically to the accumulation of private capital. One dangerous consequence is the emergence of right-wing, anti-democratic groups seeking what they regard as a just redistribution of power in their own interests.

To be sure, the picture is not categorically bleak. After 115 years the Canadian constitution was amended in 1982 to include a Charter of Rights and Freedoms comparable to the U.S. Bill of Rights. Much of the constitutional argument during the 1980s concerned the democratic future of the unelected Senate and the Supreme Court. Popular forces even demanded (unsuccessfully) the inclusion of a social contract to balance the charter's emphasis on individual rights and guarantee collective social rights in an amended constitution. Electoral participation in Canada is normally a healthy 75 percent federally (though in the 1997 election it fell to 67 percent, lowest in seventy-two years), in contrast to the U.S. rate of 50 percent or less, and there are five political parties represented in Parliament. The involvement of women, indigenous peoples, and minority groups in the political system has increased measurably over twenty years, and there remains strong pressure to extend their participation in all public institutions.

What is absent now, in contrast to the past, is an organized movement or formation to give expression to the latent popular demand for greater democracy throughout the fabric of public life. Evidence of popular discontent with Canada's limited form of liberal democracy was revealed in a prominent public opinion survey in 1990 which found that 66 percent of Canadians believed that "our whole system of government in this country" needed either "fundamental overhaul" (34 percent) or "a lot of improvement" (32 percent). A further 29 percent said the system "needed some improvement" while only 4 percent said it "basically works well." At the same time 86 percent agreed that "if governments worked properly, they could solve most of the problems Canada faces." As Leo Panitch interprets this information, "Far from being cynical, people appear to be searching for a deeper, a richer, a truer form of democracy."[2]

The failure to amend the constitution during the 1980s provides further evidence of public dissatisfaction with the form and content of Canadian democracy. The first attempt at reaching a compromise satisfactory to Quebec, the Meech Lake Agreement, was defeated by the refusal of two provincial legislatures to ratify the proposal unanimously in 1990. Interestingly, in Manitoba it was a lone indigenous member of the NDP, reflecting the anger at his people's exclusion from the agreement, who refused to supply the required unanimity; what was missing was entrenched recognition of indigenous peoples' rights to self-government. A second attempt, the 1992 Charlottetown Accord, was rejected by a popular referendum. Much of the opposition explicitly condemned the elitist, top-down approach of governments and political parties to the making of such critical public policy. A government commission that conducted wide-ranging grassroots hearings on constitution-amending in 1991 reported:

> Overwhelmingly, participants have told us that they have lost faith in the political system and its leadership. Anger, disillusion and desire for fundamental change is [sic] very often the first issue raised in discussion groups, and usually produces unanimous agreement. . . . There is no apparent regional variation in the identification of this as a major issue facing the country. Canadians are telling us that their leaders must understand and accept their vision of the country—that their leaders must be governed by the wishes of the people and not the other way around.[3]

During the public debate on amendments, citizens' groups were involved as never before in Canadian constitutional reform, and the *Globe and Mail* reported:

> . . . the current round of constitutional talks has prompted a passionate public response of a scale and intensity previously unknown in a Canadian political debate. From coast to coast feminists, trade unionists, environmentalists, students, social activists, writers, artists and many others have hammered out sophisticated proposals and brought them to the debate. For the first time, these activists—who broadly represent as many as 10 million Canadians—have insisted on defining their community values in a social charter; they have outlined a revolutionary history of Canada's origins and have drawn up a national priority list that makes economic development secondary to the social and cultural goals it might serve.[4]

There was, of course, no social charter included in the Charlottetown Accord, which accounts in part for its defeat in the referendum. But neither did any organization result from this popular mobilization for continuing and extending democracy in Canadian public life. The only political party likely to lead such a movement for greater democracy is the NDP, but it has earned few credentials for extending democracy where it does govern. Popular skepticism that it might provide such leadership was expressed in the 1993 federal election, which decimated its parliamentary standing. Though the 1997 election of twenty-one MPs restored the NDP's party status, its 11 percent popular vote was scarcely a ringing endorsement.

The Canadian state has historically exerted decisive influence in the definition and defense of an otherwise precarious national existence. The capitalist reconstruction called globalization is producing a new conventional wisdom that the nation-state is no longer capable of controlling or marshaling economic or even legal instruments for domestic purposes. Capital and the power it commands are now said to be so truly international that governance of the nation-state itself is becoming less workable. This ideological gambit is not yet popularly accepted in Canada, but there is no doubt that all political parties behave as if it were so.

To a formidable extent, Wall Street bond and currency traders and their assessments of creditworthiness have become dominant in the political calculations of federal and provincial governments in Canada. For example, in the weeks preceding the presentation of the federal budget in February 1995, the *Wall Street Journal* commented adversely on the size of Canada's debt and the economy's reliance on foreign capital investment as a cause for the weak dollar, calling Canada an "honorary third world country." Moody's bond-rating service announced the likely reduction of Canada's triple-A credit rating if the budget were not tough enough. Toward the end of March, after the budget was announced, Moody assessors arrived in Ottawa for confidential meetings prior to pronouncing judgment.[5]

Trade unions and a wide range of popular groups regularly mount determined resistance to the development of such an exclusively pro-business political ideology. Yet while they have been successful in identifying the deficiencies of liberal democracy, they have not as yet found a way to unite in a movement or party that takes the expansion of popular democracy as its goal. As Paul Sweezy said in an address in 1994:

It would be foolish to underestimate the seriousness of the defeat the opposition [to capitalist hegemony] has suffered, but it would be even more foolish to conclude that it is dead. The truth is that it is alive even if not well, and the fact that the conditions . . . that gave rise to its existence in the first place continue to operate, only more so, guarantees that it will stage a comeback as new generations of exploited and oppressed take the place of those who die or retire.

This renewal will take time. The institutional forms of the old opposition—mass organizations, political parties, sovereign states—will mostly disappear and be replaced by new ones.[6]

As these comments suggest, it is not adequate merely to defend and reaffirm liberal institutions, practices, and policies designed for the problems and opportunities of the past. Leo Panitch argues that what is needed is neither more nor less state involvement in the Canadian economy and society but a different kind of state. Events of the past two decades confirm that the Westminster parliamentary model in a federal Canada does not satisfy the requirements of democracy. Panitch finds inadequate even the limited attempts to reform it:

It is clear that when people, both those who work in the state and those who depend on its services, say they want a "fundamental overhaul" or a "lot of improvement" in "our whole system of government," they are not mainly concerned with the division of powers between federal and provincial levels of government as they are presently structured. They are reaching for something that is in fact far more fundamental, having to do with the way in which the state touches, or doesn't touch, on their everyday lives, on their capacities to realize themselves as social beings. To effect the kinds of fundamental changes that would establish a developmental democracy would require a coherent popular movement that would mobilize people's thinking and energies in this direction.[7]

Such an agenda for Canada in the twenty-first century may remind us of what the great American sociologist Robert Lynd wrote in 1957, when the Cold War had crushed the fragile attempt of the 1930s to extend American democracy:

The central problem of democracy in our time is the need to discover and use the enormous potential of democratic power. . . . If this is to be made to happen it cannot be done by mere additions to, or by re-combinations or intensifications of, liberal democratic assumptions and practices. This is not, for instance, simply a matter of "voting better men into office" or of trying harder to "safeguard our freedoms." For it is precisely the conditions of democratic freedom that are involved. To meet this issue requires the rebuilding of men's social relations from the social structure up and throughout the institutions by which the society lives. And for this to happen will require the development and application of a thoroughgoing, positive theory of democratic power by which free men will be able to control and to order together all institutional means that can contribute to their collective welfare.[8]

It is a tragedy not just for the United States but for the entire world that there was—and remains—no organized vehicle to embrace this task of establishing a positive definition of democratic power. Instead, the flourishing of imperial majesty became the American dream and reality, with grotesque consequences for the globe. Some in Canada have profited from dependence upon that imperialism, but it has caused the country as a whole to develop in a stunted and distorted fashion. Now, within the grip of a worldwide capitalist restructuring, only a class, gender, and nationality strategy that reasserts a vision of solidarity—a historic characteristic of Canadian political culture—can offer a means for imagining a different twenty-first century.

Notes

Chapter 1

1. *New York Times,* 12 February 1995. In 1996, the World Trade Organization expressed concern over the growing economic dependence of Canada on its U.S. market. The United States is the market for 80 percent of Canada's exports ($79 billion in 1996-1997) and 67 percent of its imports ($67 billion in 1996-1997). Industry Canada estimated that 45 percent of bilateral trade is intracompany trade between U.S. parents and their Canadian subsidiaries. See Madelaine Drohan, "Dependency on U.S. Leaves Canada 'Vulnerable': WTO," *Globe and Mail,* 20 November 1996.

2. See *Mike: The Memoirs of the Right Honorouble Lester B. Pearson* (Toronto: University of Toronto Press, 1973), vol. 2, chap. 10; Geoffrey A. H. Pearson, *Seize the Day: Pearson and Crisis Diplomacy* (Ottawa: Carleton University Press, 1993), chap. 9; Peter Stursberg, *Lester Pearson and the American Dilemma* (Toronto: Doubleday Canada, 1980), chap. 7.

3. "U.S. hunter groups are being urged not to come to Canada to hunt if the legislation is passed. U.S. citizens are estimated to spend about $500-million a year in Canada on hunting and fishing. The Sportsmen Conservationists of Texas and the League of Kentucky Sportsmen, Inc., already have said they will urge their members not to cross the border. The Saskatchewan Wildlife Federation pledged some months ago that, if the firearms registry becomes law, 'we will do everything in our power to convince U.S. sportsmen not to hunt or fish in Saskatchewan in 1995'." Michael Valpy, "The U.S. Cavalry Is Called In on Gun Control," *Globe and Mail,* 7 April 1995.

4. Mark Kingwell, "Why America Is the Exception and Not the Rule," *Globe and Mail,* 15 June 1996.

5. Foreign control of nonfinancial industries in Canada peaked in the late 1960s. Since then the foreign-controlled share of assets and revenues has

fallen by a third. In 1988 foreign-controlled ownership rose to 26 percent in nonfinancial industries. In energy it fell to 40 percent in 1983, then rose to 60 percent in 1988. Foreign control of revenue rose to 27 percent in 1988, well below the historic high of 46.8 percent in 1969. The U.S. portion was less than 20 percent for the 1980s. The foreign-controlled share of taxable income was 35 percent ($14.8 billion) in 1988, down from the 1975 peak of 53 percent. These figures are compiled from Statistics Canada records. In 1995, U.S. direct investment in Canada was about $113 billion, but Canadian investment in the United States had grown to $76 billion. More significantly, U.S. citizens hold $29 billion worth of Canadian stocks, but Canadians hold $44 billion worth of U.S. stocks. See Murray Campbell, "Nationalism Dips at Dawn of Global Era," *Globe and Mail,* 1 July 1997.

6. The precise number of jobs lost since the introduction of the free trade agreements is subject to continuing debate, as is the precise causal responsibility of the agreements themselves. What is beyond dispute is the guarantees from advocates of free trade that such agreements would assure retention of Canadian jobs and generate new jobs in the future. Those guarantees, and the agency of free trade in creating jobs, have yet to be fulfilled.

7. In July 1997 British Columbia fishing boats blockaded an Alaskan state ferry in a Canadian port. The issue illustrated a series of conflicts endemic to capitalism and the state. Driven by self-interest and competition, both Canadian and American fishers have been plundering the salmon stocks for many years with scant concern for the environmental effects. A regulatory agreement between West Coast and national governments in 1985, which sought to apportion the catch of migratory salmon, could not be enforced due to the power of local interests. In 1997, the Alaskan fishers, by their own admission, harvested six times their usual catch of sockeye bound for Canada. After the Canadian fishers created an international incident with the blockade, Canadian authorities, petrified at the prospect of U.S. retaliations, attacked them with all the vigor of injured U.S. interests. In a *Globe and Mail* editorial (22 July 1997), the NDP premier of British Columbia was called "Rambo" and the fishers "pirates." An unnamed Canadian official in Washington said, "There were a lot of very busy people over the weekend [trying to prevent retaliation]. These guys [Americans] have so many ways to slap us around it isn't funny. . . ." Meanwhile, in the prime minister's office, there was fury "about the noise coming from one of the provinces [British Columbia]. His [Premier Clark's] encouragement of the blockade was counterproductive," according to a member of the foreign minister's inner circle. Clark

independently threatened to cancel the lease for an underwater torpedo-testing range at Nanoose Bay used jointly by U.S. and Canadian military. This prompted Canadian officials in Ottawa and Washington to declare that Clark would not be allowed to make good on his threat which might ". . . damage a diverse security and defence relationship." See Paul Koring, "Heat Turned Down on Salmon Stew; Ferry Blockade May Have Backfired," *Globe and Mail*, 23 July 1997.

8. Leo Panitch, "Globalization and the State," in Ralph Miliband and Leo Panitch, eds., *Socialist Register 1994* (London: Merlin Press, 1994), 89-90. Panitch quotes from Greg Albo, "'Competitive Austerity' and the Impasse of Capitalist Employment Policy," in ibid., 144-70.

Chapter 2

1. Vikings established settlements in 1000, but they did not lead to permanent European occupation.
2. R. Cole Harris and John Warkentin, *Canada Before Confederation* (New York: Oxford University Press, 1974), 25.
3. Ibid., 111.
4. In the formative period between 1763 and 1791 boundaries and names changed drastically. In 1763 the territory of Quebec reached from the mouth of the St. Lawrence to the Great Lakes. In 1774 it was extended from the Labrador Sea south to the Ohio River and west to include all of the Great Lakes. But with the constitution of 1791 it was reduced again and renamed Lower Canada, next to Upper Canada (later Ontario).
5. H. McD. Clokie, *Canadian Government and Politics* (Toronto: Longmans, Green, 1944), 22.
6. Greg Keilty, *1837: Revolution in the Canadas* (Toronto: NC Press, 1974), 9.
7. In the 1990s, the Northwest Territories were divided between east and west, the eastern portion named Nunavut.
8. V. C. Fowke, *The National Policy and the Wheat Economy* (Toronto: University of Toronto Press, 1957), chap. 1.
9. Evelyn Dumas, *The Bitter Thirties in Quebec* (Montreal: Black Rose Books, 1975), 19-20.
10. Conrad Black, *Duplessis* (Toronto: McClelland and Stewart, 1977).
11. J. F. Conway, *The West* (Toronto: James Lorimer, 1984), 99.

Chapter 3

1. F. H. Leacy, ed., *Historical Statistics of Canada*, second edition (Ottawa: Statistics Canada, 1983), G191, G192.

2. J. W. Warnock, *Partner to Behemoth* (Toronto: New Press, 1970), 107.
3. Ibid., 121.
4. Melissa Clark-Jones, *A Staple State* (Toronto: University of Toronto Press, 1987), 12-21.
5. U.S. productions account for about 70 percent of all television viewing in English Canada. U.S. feature films account for about 95 percent of the theater distribution in English Canada and 83 percent in Quebec. Before 1970, there was no Canadian music industry. In 1971, Canadian content regulations were introduced in the broadcast industry, with the result that today the Canadian recording industry accounts for about 13 percent of annual recording sales. Prior to 1976, Canadian journals accounted for just 34 million circulation. After that date, the Canadian magazine industry came into existence when the government enacted legislation to prevent U.S. magazines from skimming advertising with split runs. In publishing, too, it was government policies that sheltered the growth of an almost extinct industry in the 1970s with measures to regulate foreign ownership and various financial assistance programs. Murray Campbell, "Canadian Culture, Then and Now," *Globe and Mail,* 1 July 1997.

Chapter 4

1. Lorne and Caroline Brown, *An Unauthorized History of the RCMP* (Toronto: James Lewis & Samuel, 1973), 41-42.
2. *Monitor* (Ottawa) 2, no. 5 (October 1995).
3. Leo Panitch and Donald Swartz, *The Assault on Trade Union Freedoms* (Toronto: Garamond Press, 1993), appendix I.
4. Sam Gindin and David Robertson, "Alternatives to Competitiveness," in Daniel Drache, ed., *Getting on Track* (Montreal: McGill-Queen's University Press, 1992), 37-38.

Chapter 5

1. Paradoxically, the Parti Quebecois government of the 1990s has returned to union pension funds to alleviate its budget deficit problems, but now under the regimen of program cutbacks.
2. Bombardier is a diversified heavy industrial equipment company that has grown to international proportions from its Quebec base. Quoted in Kenneth McRoberts and Dale Postgate, *Quebec: Social Change and Political Crisis* (Toronto: McClelland and Stewart, 1980), 201.
3. Roy Romanow, et al., *Canada Notwithstanding; The Making of the Constitution 1976-1982* (Toronto: Carswell/Methuen, 1984), chap. 7.

4. Rheal Seguin, "Separatism's New Siren Call," *Globe and Mail,* 7 May 1994: D1, 2.
5. Rheal Seguin, "Parizeau Scathes Corporate Quebec," *Globe and Mail,* 4 October 1995.
6. Rheal Seguin, "Yes, and the Move to the Left," *Globe and Mail,* 28 October 1995.

Chapter 6

1. Tom Naylor, "The History of Democratic and Foreign Capital in Canada," in Canada, Ltd.: The Political Economy of Dependency, ed. Robert M. Laxer (Toronto: McClelland and Stewart, 1973), 45.
2. Samuel Yellen, *American Labor Stuggles* (New York: S. A. Russell, 1956), 244ff.
3. Lorne Brown, *When Freedom was Lost; The Unemployed, the Agitator and the State* (Montreal: Black Rose Books, 1987).
4. Michael Mandel, *The Charter of Rights and the Legalization of Politics in Canada* (Toronto: Thompson Educational Publishing, 1994).
5. Edward Greenspon, "Smaller is Better in New-Look Ottawa," *Globe and Mail,* 28 February 1995.
6. Nicos Poulantzas, *Classes in Contemporary Capitalism* (London: New Left Books, 1975), 73, quoted in Leo Panitch, "Globalization and the State," in Miliband and Panitch, eds., *Socialist Register 1994* (London: Merlin Press, 1994), 67.
7. Panitch, ibid.
8. Ibid., 75, emphasis in original.

Chapter 7

1. The oxymoron "Progressive Conservative" was adopted in the late 1930s, when the Conservative Party sought to attract rural supporters of the short lived Progressive Party.
2. "Canadians Content, Survey Finds," *Globe and Mail,* 16 March 1994.
3. "Discussion Papers, Des Documents de Discussion," CAW/TCA, 4th Constitutional Convention, the Quebec Convention Centre, Quebec City, P.Q., 23-26 August 1994, 8.
4. Leo Panitch and David Swartz, *The Assault on Trade Union Freedoms* (Toronto: Garamond Press, 1993), 156.
5. William K. Tabb, "Globalization is *an* Issue, the Power of Capital is *the* Issue," *Monthly Review* 49, no. 2 (June 1997): 26.

Chapter 8

1. C. D. Howe was a business tycoon, government bureaucrat, and Liberal politician whose wartime role as mobilization czar and strategist was similar to that of Bernard Baruch in the United States.
2. David Langille, "The Business Council on National Issues and the Canadian State," *Studies in Political Economy* no. 24 (Autumn 1987): 41-85.
3. *Monitor* 1, no. 8 (February 1995): 15.

Chapter 9

1. In 1974 there were 264 seats in Parliament.
2. Leo Panitch and Donald Swartz, *The Assault on Trade Union Freedoms: From Wage Controls to Social Contract* (Toronto: Garamond Press, 1993), 170.
3. Ibid., 179.

Chapter 10

1. Daniel Singer, "Europe's Crisis," *Monthly Review* 46, no. 3 (July-August 1994): 93, 95.
2. Leo Panitch, "A Different Kind of State?" in *A Different Kind of State? Popular Power and Democratic Administrations,* ed. Gregory Albo, David Langille, and Leo Panitch (New York: Oxford University Press, 1993), 3.
3. Citizens' Forum on Canada's Future, *Theme Reports: A Working Paper* (Ottawa: Supply and Services Canada, 1991), 8, cited in Panitch, "A Diffferent Kind of State?," 4.
4. Linda Hossie, "Grassroots Groups altered content of Unity Debate," *Globe and Mail,* 25 February 1992.
5. "Bankrupt Canada?," *Wall Street Journal,* 12 January 1995; "Canada's Rating in Jeopardy," *Globe and Mail,* 17 February 1995.
6. Paul Sweezy, "*Monthly Review* in Historical Perspective," *Monthly Review* 45, no. 8 (January 1994): 7.
7. Panitch, "A Different Kind of State?," 9.
8. R. S. Lynd, "Power in American Society as Resource and Problem," in A. Kornhauser, ed., *Problems of Power in American Democracy* (Detroit: Wayne State University Press, 1957), 44-45.

Bibliography

Albo, Gregory, David Langille, and Leo Panich, eds. *A Different Kind of State?: Popular Power and Democratic Administration.* Toronto: Oxford University Press, 1993.

Angus, Ian. *Canadian Bolsheviks: An Early History of the Communist Party of Canada.* Montreal: Vanguard Publications, 1981.

Brodie, Janine and Jane Jenson. *Crisis, Challenge and Change: Party and Class in Canada Revisited.* Ottawa: Carleton University Press, 1988.

Cameron, Duncan and Mel Watkins, eds. *Canada Under Free Trade.* Toronto: Harcourt Brace and Jovanovich , 1993.

Clarke, Tony. *Silent Coup: Confronting the Big Business Takeover of Canada.* Toronto: James Lorimer and Company / Ottawa: Canadian Centre for Policy Alternatives, 1997.

Clark-Jones, Melissa. *A Staple State: Canadian Industrial Resources in Cold War.* Toronto: University of Toronto Press, 1987.

Clement, Wallace and Glen Williams, eds. *The New Canadian Political Economy.* Montreal: McGill-Queen's University Press, 1989. A comprehensive bibliography of Canadian political economy since the 1960s.

Clement, Wallace. *Class Power and Property: Essays on Canadian Society.* Toronto, New York: Methuen, 1983.

Finkel, Alvin. *Business and Social Reform in the Thirties.,* Toronto: James Lorimer and Company, 1979.

Forbes, Ernest R. and D. A. Muise, eds. *The Atlantic Provinces in Confederation.* Toronto: University of Toronto Press , 1993.

Fowke, Vernon C. *The National Policy and the Wheat Economy.* Toronto: University of Toronto Press, 1957.

Greenspun, Ricardo and M. A. Cameron, eds. *The Political Economy of North American Free Trade*. Montreal: McGill-Queen's University Press / Ottawa: Canadian Centre for Policy Alternatives, 1993.

Guest, Dennis. *The Emergence of Social Security in Canada*. 3d ed. Vancouver: University of British Columbia Press, 1997.

Heron, Craig. *The Canadian Labour Movement*. Toronto: James Lorimer and Company, 1996.

Kealy, Linda and Joan Sangster, eds. *Beyond the Vote: Canadian Women and Politics*. Toronto: University of Toronto Press, 1989.

Laux, Jeanne Kirk and Maureen Appel Molot. *State Capitalism: Public Enterprise in Canada*. Ithaca, N.Y.: Cornell University Press, 1988.

Laxer, James and Robert Laxer. *The Liberal Idea of Canada: Pierre Trudeau and the Question of Canada's Survival*. Toronto: James Lorimer and Company, 1977.

Laycock, David. *Populism and Democratic Thought in the Canadian Prairies, 1910 to 1945*. Toronto: University of Toronto Press, 1990.

Lower, Arthur R. M. *Colony to Nation: A History of Canada*. Montreal: Longmans Canada, 1964.

McRoberts, Kenneth. *Misconceiving Canda: The Struggle for National Unity*. Toronto: Oxford University Press, 1997.

Naylor, R. T. *Canada in the European Age, 1453-1919*. Vancouver: New Star Books, 1987.

———. *The History of Canadian Business, 1867-1914*, vol. I: *The Banks and Finance Capital;* vol.II: *Industrial Development*. Toronto: James Lorimer and Company, 1975.

Niosi, Jorge. *The Economy of Canada: A Study of Ownership and Control*. Montreal: Black Rose Press, 1978.

Panitch, Leo and Donald Swartz. *The Assault on Trade Union Freedoms*. Toronto: Garamond Press, 1993.

Penner, Norman. *From Protest to Power: Social Democracy in Canada 1900-Present*. Toronto: James Lorimer and Company, 1992.

Pentland, H. Clare, *Labour and Capital in Canada 1650-1860,* Toronto: James Lorimer and Company.[PUB DATE????]

Ryerson, Stanley B. *Unequal Union: Confederation and the Roots of Conflict in the Canadas, 1815-1873*. New York: International Publishers, 1968.

_____. *The Founding of Canada: Beginnings to 1815*. Toronto: Progress Books, 1975.

Teeple, Gary, 1995, *Globalization and the Decline of Social Reform*, Toronto: Garamond Press.

Whitaker, Reg and Gary Marcuse. *Cold War Canada: The Making of a National Insecurity State, 1945-1957*. Toronto: University of Toronto Press, 1994.

Index